GHOSTS OF EAST BERLIN

ERIC FRIEDMAN

WITH

CELESTE MCCONNELL-BARBER

ISBN: 1501004611
ISBN-13: 978-1501004612

DEDICATION

For Frank
(1942 – 1999)

Our Odysseus
"To strive, to seek, to find, and not to yield."

CONTENTS

ACKNOWLEDGMENTS

The authors wish to acknowledge those good friends with whom we shared the frustrations and delights of life in our Berlin.

Frank's colleagues and students at Humboldt University: Professor Christopher Mueller, Professor Horst Ihda. Their students, including Christina and Frank's "silly girls."

Our fellow Americans: Liz, David, Ann and Ralph, and also the Solomons. Keith Barlow, the British Socialist living one floor below (and an apologist for Stalin).

Our Berliner friends, who regularly crossed over borders to extend their love and friendship: Gerlinde, Heike, Jurgen, and beloved Addi. Eric's young friends, too: Epi, George and Dezso.

Finally, our Berlin. As ever, she is the central city of the world and the imagination. Haunted and haunting.

Auf Wiedersehen, old Berlin.

INTRODUCTION

Council for International Exchange of Scholars

Eleven Dupont Circle, N.W. • Washington, D.C. 20036-1257
Affiliated with the American Council of Learned Societies

February 4, 1987

Barbara S. Uehling
Chancellor
University of California, Santa Barbara
5221 Cheadle Hall
Santa Barbara, CA 93106

Dear Chancellor Uehling:

It gives me great pleasure to inform you that a member of your faculty, Frank D. McConnell, Department of English, has received a Fulbright grant to the German Democratic Republic. I am delighted that your faculty member has been so honored, and am sure that the Fulbright experience will have far-reaching benefits for your institution.

The Fulbright grants, which are awarded on the basis of a national competition, represent a significant part of the federal government's commitment to international educational exchange. As you may know, all Fulbright applications undergo rigorous peer review, a process that is conducted by the Council for International Exchange of Scholars.

While this award is conferred on an individual scholar, the grantee's experience abroad as a lecturer or researcher can be of great value to your own institution. I am impressed with the creative ways many Fulbright scholars have shared their international experience with colleagues and students and I urge all institutions to take special note of the enhanced skills and broadened experience of the returned Fulbrighter. With this in mind, I would ask you to pass this letter on to your appropriate academic officer and encourage that some occasions be created for Dr. McConnell to share the benefits of the Fulbright grant on return to your campus.

I am confident that, with your support, your institution will continue to benefit from the broadened international dimension that characterizes the Fulbright program.

My very good wishes.

Sincerely,

Cassandra A. Pyle
Executive Director

cc: Frank D. McConnell

FULBRIGHT ACCEPTANCE LETTER.

ERIC

GOODBYE AMERICA HELLO BERLIN

FULL CIRCLE

Growing up, I was an only child who was painfully shy. I towered above most other kids my age while remaining half their weight. This meant I literally stood out and did everything I could to not be noticed, for as much as we adults romanticize childhood, it can be very brutal. In my case, I was the model for *Diary of a Wimpy Kid*. This physical awkwardness led me to be very quiet yet constantly observant of my surroundings. I was fearful of change because it took great time and effort for me to develop friendships with kids I could trust and avoid being noticed by everyone else. With this being the case, I was terrified of going to Berlin and fully despised my mom, Frank and the rest of my family for forcing me to go. I knew that not only would I no longer be anonymous, I would be the center of attention.

As it turns out, Berlin taught me many truths about life, most of which went unnoticed at the time, but were revealed to me when I was ready to understand them. Looking back and reflecting on those truly extraordinary months, I now recognize how Berlin changed the trajectory of my life and continues to influence me to this very day. Berlin offered me a global experience at a time when my world view was that of my neighborhood. Berlin also forced me to face many of my fears while giving me the confidence to both understand and overcome them. Now, a quarter century later, I celebrate the decision of my mom, Frank and the rest of my family. They knew what was best for that scared ten year old kid from so long ago and this 36 year old man is forever in their debt.

GOODBYE AMERICA

The scene at Los Angeles International Airport on that warm January morning of 1988 will forever be etched in my mind. It was the first of only two occasions in my life in which members of both sides of my family were gathered in the same place, the second being my high school graduation seven years later. Being only ten years old at the time, it was a moment that I never wanted to end. Since I was a small child I had dreamed about a time when my mom, dad, grandparents, aunts, uncles and cousins were all together and it had finally come true. However, this was not the happy occasion I had envisioned, for in two hours my mom Celeste, step-father Frank, and I would be on a plane to East Berlin, the city at the heart of the "Evil Empire." It was just six months after President Reagan challenged Gorbachev to "tear down this Wall." The historical significance of Berlin mattered little to me. All I knew was we would be gone for six months, which is an eternity for a ten-year-old.

We were there because of Frank. He was a distinguished English professor at U.C. Santa Barbara, but without the pretentious assholishness (is that even a word) that English professors are legendary for possessing. In contrast, his personality was larger than life and he always brought people together for no greater reason than to break bread. Frank was famous for cracking profane jokes, his proficient yet non-profane manner of infusing F-Bombs into any conversation, and most importantly, taking a sincere interest in the stories of the people and the world around him. I suppose that last characteristic, more than any other, was why he was selected for the teaching gig at Humboldt University in East Berlin.

Frank's knowledge of the English canon and understanding of the human condition was second to none. And, appropriately, he physically resembled that famous picture of Albert Einstein sticking his tongue out, down to the crazy hair and large bushy moustache.

Among the ailments he possessed were a smokers' cough, a small but growing beer belly, weak ankles and an occasional case of gout. Since he was afraid to go to the doctor, he walked with a cane, partly to relieve the pressure and partly for dramatic effect. In both his looks and his brilliance, I have determined Frank to be proof that alternative universes do exist. In our universe, Einstein lived as a wild eyed English Professor with Irish lineage who grew up in Louisville, Kentucky; who left to see the world and never looked back. However, on this particular, I sincerely wished he had left my universe alone.

That morning, the three of us and the rest of my family were gathered in one of the many restaurants at LAX located adjacent to our departure gate. All of us were silently counting down the minutes and seconds until it would be time for us to board the plane to Frankfurt. To pass the time we hid behind the comfort of meaningless conversation. These were the days of air travel prior to 9/11 which meant that your friends and family could actually accompany you to your gate and wave goodbye to you as you walked down the tarmac or, conversely, greet you as you exited the plane upon your return. The ability to see the faces of your loved ones and speak with them moments before you depart, or to experience the joy of smiles and a tight hug immediately upon your return is without a doubt the greatest loss in modern air travel. For me, these last few moments with my family, especially my dad, Herb, were to become the precious memories that would carry me through the next six months, memories that in today's world would never have been possible.

All of us were quite nervous and fearful over this trip. While Moscow may have been the brains behind the Evil Empire, Berlin was its heart and soul. The three of us were on our way, willingly, (except me) to live and interact with the sworn enemies of the United States. This fact was not lost on my grandfather Carl, who received a Purple Heart and Bronze Star in the Battle of the Bulge and was furious that his eldest daughter and grandson were going to live with the communists, even though we weren't communists and this adventure was arranged through the Council for International Exchange of Scholars and was an approved Fulbright grant. And if the tension wasn't already high enough with my Grandpa, this was also the first time the two sides of my family were face to face since my parents' divorce in 1980.

Oh, and there was the added drama that came from two hours of martini's and Xanax.

Ah, yes the Xanax, supplied by Granny Dolores, a manic personality with psychotic tendencies who juxtaposed my quiet and conservative Grandpa Carl. This day she happened (or purposefully) to have an episode. At the time she weighed about 300 pounds and chain-smoked 3 packs of Virginia Slims a day while taking a concoction of medications to combat all her neuroses. Naturally, it was she who set the tone.

Granny was handing out Xanax like it was candy on Halloween. First she gave Frank one and then offered our waitress a half a pill. I distinctly recall calculating in my head that the combined weight of Frank and the waitress, who was literally my size at five foot 2 and about a hundred pounds, was less than that of Granny. Even at my young age of 10, I knew that taking the infamous pills would not be a good idea. Needless to say, about an hour later Frank was no longer nervous, of course he could no longer walk, and the waitress was expressing her unconditional love for my Granny. She was soon replaced by another waitress never to be seen again. While this might not seem of any significance, her disappearance from the scene was a prelude to others who would disappear when they became too friendly with us.

When it was finally time to board the plane Frank was nearly passed out. My mom and I had the dual task of saying goodbye and trying to convince the airline staff to let us on the plane. They were refusing to let Frank on because they thought he was too inebriated. What they didn't understand was that he was basically asleep and would, without a doubt, be their best passenger since the Xanax would knock him out until we touched down in Frankfurt. After they agreed to let us on, I quickly hugged my grandparents, aunts, uncles, cousins and my dad.

When I hugged my dad, I began to cry because I couldn't imagine not seeing him for six months. I was also angry with him because I knew that he had the ability to tell my mom I wasn't going. I knew he could have stopped my nightmare. I hugged him as tightly as possible, praying that he or someone in my family would tell my mom and Frank to leave me here. I felt like they were all abandoning me, even my cousins who were all younger than me. Eventually the hug ended and my dad told me how much he loved me and that he would write me every week. He even joked that someday, when I was as ancient as he, I would understand two things: that six months is a lot shorter than it seems and this was a once in a lifetime journey. It turned out he was right on both accounts, and now, as a father myself, I know it was more difficult for him to let me go. I am always amazed by the perspective that the passage of time affords us.

"I will see you before you know it," he said. With that, I waved good-bye to everyone and followed my mom and Frank into the tunnel and on to the plane. The last thing I remember was sitting in my seat and looking out the window trying to see if I could see my family in the terminal, but I couldn't. It was then that I knew the day I had been dreading since the prior summer was finally here. When the plane took off I simply looked at the seat in front of me and prayed to God that my dad was right about this six months being over before I knew it. That was 25 years ago, or 50 six month intervals.

HELLO BERLIN

The six thousand mile journey from Los Angeles to Berlin had paradoxically calmed me down and increased my anxiety. Although I would still rather have left the airport with my Dad, I was now determined to make the best of my circumstances and was actually excited to experience a foreign country and specifically Berlin. I also figured it was now one day less than six months before I would return home. Unfortunately, my first impression of Berlin, which was quite mortifying, quickly tested my resolve. It also provided me with a quick lesson on the meaning of culture, its impact and how it changes from country to country.

While the America I know is a complex nation and made of culturally diverse peoples, it can also be defined largely by a single word, the acronym For Unlawful Carnal Knowledge, or "FUCK." Perhaps it is our puritan roots and the accompanying warped sense of sexuality that has made the word FUCK, in all its forms, the quintessential word in American slang and part of our collective American experience. In Germany though, the equivalent to *Fuck* is *Sheisse*, literally translated "shit." We say "fuck you", the Germans say "Ich sheisse on sie" (I shit on you). The intent is the same, but the words are a reflection of each distinct culture. As I quickly learned during my first moments in Berlin, culture and the German preference for *sheisse* rather than *fuck*, had real world consequences that both *fucked* with me and *shit* on me at the moment of my arrival.

About 20 minutes before the flight from Frankfurt to Berlin was to land my stomach started to gurgle. Unfortunately, one of my greatest phobias is having to use an airplane bathroom. Although now as an adult I could manage in a pinch, there was no way on earth at ten years old that I was going to use the inflight bathroom, no matter how badly my stomach demanded relief. On this particular day, since the flight was so close to landing, I knew I could hold out for terminal. Although not optimal, it was a much better alternative. After one of the longest half –hours of my life, including de-boarding time, we finally were standing on terra firma in West Berlin's Tegal airport. Granny's Xanax were now a distant memory and our arrival in one of the most historical cities in human history officially marked the beginning of our journey. For me, it meant I could now take care of business.

After de-boarding the plane and entering the terminal, I hurriedly walked into the men's room with my legs cramped together. I was doing the poo walk/dance and knew I had about a minute left until critical mass. Each step, if not taken with care and caution could lead to disaster. Upon entering the men's room I couldn't believe my eyes. I found myself in the cleanest most perfect public bathroom I had ever visited! There wasn't a germ, or misplaced paper towel for miles around! I had heard rumors about the Germans' adherence to cleanliness, but this was ridiculous. This facility was more sterile than a hospital. It was the Xanadu of airport public restrooms! I breathed a huge sigh of relief and even cracked a smile. Perhaps the next six months weren't going to be so bad after all I thought. With time of the essence I stepped into the first all-black stall. Then I saw the toilet and my new found world of the perfect public restroom shattered.

Immediately I thought about Frank. He loved telling jokes, many with a punch-line stating something about European toilets. As a kid I never understood. But now I did, for the joke was on me. I was mortified to find before me a German toilet that was masquerading as an American toilet. On the outside everything was fine, but where it mattered most was a bowl of horrors. Instead of having a deep bowl with plenty of water, there was a small raised platform in the center of the bowl that had only about an inch of water. How was I supposed to shit in an inch of water I asked myself? With time running out, I quickly went to a second stall, then a third, hoping for a miracle, but instead, I ran out of time.

Those few minutes sitting on a German toilet were the first of many life lessons Berlin was going to teach me. With my feces piling up below me I learned some valuable insights into human nature. Perhaps the most significant is that as human beings we try to be neat and proper, yet we are naturally attracted to chaos and things that make us cringe. In my case, while I was mortified about having to use this toilet, I couldn't help but periodically look down. It was like trying not to stare at the fatal accident on the highway when you drive by. Try as you might, you always look. Eventually, when my intestine emptied itself and I had finished wiping my ass, it was time to flush. No matter how hard I tried, I was compelled by forces greater than myself to look down at my own excrement, covered in toilet paper, completely out of the water. It was as if it was designed to be in this condition, just for me to observe before I flushed. As it turns out, it was.

When I exited the bathroom, I had this perplexed look on my face. My mom and Frank laughed as I described the toilet debacle. Frank, who was a human encyclopedia, eventually explained to me that the German toilet was a remnant to pre-sanitation days in which people had to look at their feces in order to tell if there was a sickness or other condition that needed to be addressed. He also taught me that Germans are very precise, or anal, and nothing could be out of place, especially in their shit. This obsessiveness with cleanliness and order had real world ramifications which includes German culture using the word *shit* rather than *fuck* as the alpha slang word. If you think about it though, for a culture obsessed with cleanliness, shitting on someone is a far more demeaning statement than fucking someone.

As a post script to my experience in Tegal Airport, there was an added bonus that occurred once we found ourselves on the other side of the Wall. In East Berlin there were very few natural resources, which caused shortages of essential goods. This lack of resources was compounded by a government that decried the luxuries of the West. The resulting consequences were a lack of essential foods such as fruits and vegetables and other convenience items. Unfortunately, convenience items included soft toilet paper. Upon arriving at our apartment in the East Berlin suburb of Marzahn, we discovered the same German toilet with the one inch trough, but it was accompanied by a roll of toilet paper that felt more like 100 grit sandpaper. We were fortunate my mom had planned ahead and packed a few rolls of toilet paper. We made it last until our first trip to West Berlin. Over the next six months, nothing became more valuable than civilized toilet paper. As we made friends through our stay we would make it a point to offer them a roll or two. When they felt it for the first time, you would have thought they were in heaven.

FRIENDSHIP

KATARINA WITT

On December 6, 1956 the Hungarian Water Polo Team defeated the Soviet Union 4-0 to win Olympic Gold in a match termed "Blood in the Water." The Gold Medal match came just weeks after Soviet tanks violently rolled through Budapest to suppress the growing threat of a Hungarian revolt for independence. When the carnage was done, over 2,500 lives were lost and thousands more injured. This series of events came to define the political theater that made the Olympics some of the most intriguing and historically significant aspects of the Cold War.

With images of the Soviet invasion still fresh in their minds, the Gold Medal match provided the Hungarians a chance for revenge. Conversely, the Soviets knew a defeat of the Hungarians would land a crushing blow with ramifications felt from Moscow to Budapest to Washington D.C. The "Blood in the Water" match defined what a Gold Medal truly meant, all the way to the final Cold War Olympics of 1988.

By 1988, the theater had shifted from the brutality of "blood in the water" to the spectacle of "the beauty on ice." After the U.S. boycott in 1980 and the Soviet boycott of 1984 the tensions were high, and the world was anticipating the Superpower showdown of 1988. In America we were all standing behind our athletes and prepared to go to war against the Evil Empire. Our entire country knew that every Gold medal was a not only a victory for America but a triumph of democracy and our values of freedom over those of the Soviet Union and communism. Like the Hungarians in 1956, our athletes had the opportunity to do what our diplomats and Department of Defense could not: kick their ass and put them in their place. As our family quickly learned from our vantage point in East Berlin, the feeling was mutual.

Shortly after we arrived in Berlin, the 1988 Winter Olympics began. As the games unfolded and we watched the East German coverage on our black and white television, we realized how important the games were to both the Soviets and the other countries under their rule, but for different reasons. The games for the Soviets had the same connotations as here in the United States. Every gold medal they won, or that their bloc won, was a victory for their political and social philosophy. It was a fight for supremacy that combined their forces, along with those of East Germany and China, in a battle against the United States, Britain, West Germany and France. However, there was the intriguing subplot of the Soviet Bloc countries, most notably East Germany, who also desired to kick the Soviets' ass. For them, a gold medal was a triumph over both the world superpowers and their rival West Germans. It was three decades later and the contagious fire of the Hungarian revolution from the '56 games had never been fully extinguished.

My folks and I would anticipate the Olympic drama every night. Besides being one of the few programs we could watch due to the language barrier, the games also gave the three of us some comfort and sense of home in knowing that all of our friends and family back in the U.S. were watching the same events as we were, although in color. However, even though I was just 10 years old, I knew my version and experience of these games was different from my friends and family back home, and not just because I was aware of the significance of the politics surrounding the games. It was different because of Katarina Witt.

I knew she was a hated East German, but I couldn't help but be mesmerized by her. Every time there was a close up of her smiling on our tiny T.V., I imagined she was smiling at me. I couldn't wait to turn on the T.V. each night and welcome her into our home. For the first time in my life, I had a physical reaction, an anxiety in a sense, when I saw her. It was so bad that I couldn't bear to watch her skate because of my own fear for her. Her power over me was so great that before I knew it, I had transformed into an East German and, at least in Figure Skating, found myself rooting against the Americans! But, it wasn't just me who fell in love with her.

Katarina was the darling of East Germany. With her stunning beauty and unmatched agility on the ice, she single-handedly woke the sleepy colorless East Berlin from its winter slumber and created an excitement that burned through the thick Soviet fog that blanketed the city. For those few weeks we couldn't go anywhere without hearing her name and seeing the lit up smiles on the faces of East Berliners who suddenly walked with an extra kick in their step and possessed a newly found upright posture. With each step toward the gold, she became more myth than reality. Her victories on the ice and her love for the people of East Germany brought a true sense of hope to its people. Berliners were united in their cheering for her, and for the only time in our experience in the City, there was no fear, no intimidation, no worry of saying the wrong thing and suddenly disappearing. Katarina, for those brief few weeks set the people of East Berlin free. It was in these moments of citywide joy, while lost in my own daydreams of her, that I realized the Olympics have a completely different meaning for other countries.

We noticed this difference in many ways, especially in how the games were televised. Katarina was always shown in the best possible manner. She was constantly smiling and full of energy. She never had an awkward moment. But whenever they showed the Americans, especially Debi Thomas who was Katarina's American competition, there was an indifferent frown. In fact, it seemed that when they weren't showing Katarina, they had a close up of Debi who always looked as if she was pissed off and didn't want to be there. The three of us used to laugh out loud at the absurdity of the coverage and then scream at Debi to smile. I couldn't believe nor understand that she didn't know she was being used as a communist propaganda machine. "Don't you know they're watching you!" I would yell to no avail.

The East German government used both Katarina and Debi to fit their narrative of the great East triumphing over the morally bankrupt West. It was too easy, the truth be damned! It was the narrative above all else that mattered. To know what was real, we didn't have to think for ourselves, all we had to do was look at the story as it unfolded on our T.V. and witness an East German goddess capturing the hearts of her country juxtaposed to an ungrateful American with arrogance about her who thought she was entitled to the gold. But it wasn't just the unfortunate Debi Thomas who had to compete against one of the most memorable Olympic athletes of all time, it was all Americans. The East Germans would limit the showing of American Gold, but always provided a well-timed close-up of the faces of our athletes when another country was raising the precious medal.

Of course the three of us knew that the real Debi Thomas was nothing like the one portrayed on our propaganda box. But in life, reality is what we experience, and to my folks and I, we experienced a reality where Debi Thomas never smiled and was jealous of the princess on ice, Katarina.

The culmination of this East German fairy tale concluded with a triumphant Katarina hoisting the Gold, a solemn Debi left with the Bronze and me, heartbroken, that Katarina no longer stopped by to visit.

Epi

Epi, as was told to me by him and others, remembers very little of his birth village in Namibia. Among his few recollections are he had a mother, father and an older sister who was about 5 or 6. His basic needs in the village were met, and to the best of his recollections, he never lacked shelter, food or a loving family. For the most part, that's all he remembers. He has no pictures or mementos of his family or home. No friends or relatives to help him recall, just distant memories that faded over time. They were memories that ended in unimaginable violence, the kind which wake you in the middle of the night and haunt you to your core. The kind you desperately want to forget but you can't because they are all you have left and it is better to recall the terror of your past than nothing at all. They are the kind of memories that form a lifetime of unanswerable questions starting with, "How did I even survive?"

Epi's survival is nothing short of a miracle. Sometime in 1977 or 78 a team of East German journalists led by our friend, Heike Schneider, were traveling in Namibia. By sheer chance they happened to be the first to arrive at the scene of the still smoldering village. The militia responsible was gone having left the streets lined with bodies and the air thick with smoke. As Heike and her crew documented the devastation, they also searched for survivors. First they came upon an old man sitting in a chair. He was catatonic to his surroundings. He made no recognition of their presence. In the absence of any words, the news crew began to form an understanding of what had occurred. When they moved on from the old man to search for others they found Epi.

Epi was wandering the streets alone and terrified screaming for his mom. He was wearing nothing but a soiled cloth diaper, and was covered in dirt from the roads and soot from the fires. Not knowing what to do, Heike instinctively approached Epi and was able to calm him down, slowly building trust. As Heike soothed Epi, the others continued to search the village for survivors and found others, mostly elderly and in not much better condition than the old man in the chair. Within minutes it became evident that Epi's family was murdered and there was nobody left in the village that could care for him.

As Heike and the others waited in the village for help to arrive, they continued to care for Epi while also trying to figure out what to do with him. The life of this orphaned three year old child was literally in her hands and she understood the gravity of her decision. It was at this moment that Heike was faced with an ethical dilemma that I imagine most journalists worth their salt face at some point in their career: would she continue to document the story or would she become the story? My understanding of journalism, especially investigative journalism, is that journalists have an unwritten code that they do not become the story. However, they must weigh this code with an equally, or perhaps more significant, human moral code, which is, we are our brother's keeper.

Heike's dilemma was that if she chose to become the story she would no longer be reporting it and therefore not fulfill her duty to accurately inform the world of what took place. The ultimate danger was that in saving one child, the world would never become outraged enough to take action and save the thousands of other children that had no journalists to document their stories. But Epi was real, literally crying in her arms. She was his only chance.

I cannot even begin to comprehend what went through Heike's thought process as she sat there in the ruins of the smoldering village with Epi in her arms knowing her decision could ultimately decide whether he lived or died. I envision it to be a process that was part rational, part instinct and part prayer. I wonder if it was the moment in her life where she answered the question of whether God exists. I suppose this question is one that all journalists will have to answer at some point. And when they do, their sanity will require them to somehow separate the journalist code from the moral code. But what happens when you can't separate the two?

Heike chose the human moral code. Over the course of the ensuing months she was able to secure the required approvals from both the authorities in Namibia and East Germany to adopt Epi and raise him in her home in East Berlin. While her decision saved Epi's life and ensured he was raised in a home where he was loved and cared for, it presented many new challenges, the most significant of which was how their family was to live and overcome racial prejudice in a country where it was forbidden by force. Through meeting Epi, and learning his story in both Namibia and Berlin, I learned first-hand about hatred and racism and how it can be overcome.

Epi and I were introduced to each other through mutual friends, the Wedels, whom we had met during our time in Berlin. Jurgen and Adelheide Wedel had known Heike Schneider for years and had been a part of Epi's life since he moved to Berlin. They had an eight year old son, George, who was close to Epi. In fact, they were more like brothers since they had grown-up together. Over the course of my six months in Berlin, the three of us were naturally drawn to each other and we became close friends.

My friendship with Epi and George was unique when compared to all other friendships I have had in my life. Being that we had no common language in which to communicate, other than my limited German and Epi's fragmented English, our other senses compensated to help us understand each other. Whether it was exaggerated body movements, or paying more attention to facial expressions, or drawing pictures, it was an absence of a common language that solidified our bond and allowed us to communicate effectively. We were forced to take extra time to learn about each other.

As the weeks went by my German improved as did Epi's English, and even George learned some English. But in the end, it was our actions, not our words, that brought us together: we ran around outside, climbed trees, built structures with Legos, played cards, laughed hysterically for no reason at all, and listened to music, the same 80's pop of Pet Shop Boys, Peter Gabriel, the Police, and DJ Jazzy Jeff and the Fresh Prince, that my friends and I listened to back in California. We were three kids with incredibly different backgrounds, yet to each other we were equals.

The significance of my childhood relationship with Epi and George, is that it established the foundation for my views on two of the most critical issues all adults must eventually face, their own prejudices in regards to hatred and race. As a child growing up in America with the backdrop of the 1980's Cold War, I was taught that the Soviet Union and the other communist countries were our enemies. Whether intended or not, the message that I received was that all people of the Soviet Bloc were communists, that they hated the United States and they would stop at nothing to take our freedom.

As impressionable kids, my friends and I literally believed the Soviet Bloc and its entire people were actually an "Evil Empire", for as a young child I was unable to distinguish between a government and its citizens. They were one and the same and it was ingrained in my head that in the United States we were a government "of the people and by the people," so naturally, other countries must also have the same connection between the government and people. From my perspective at the time, the Evil Empire was a government of an evil people by an evil people.

Of course, my friendship with Epi and George, along with other children I met during this time, changed my perception. I distinctly remember when I finally questioned my beliefs on this subject. I was confused as to how the people of East Germany could hate me and why I should hate them when "the people" were actually my friends: Epi, George and their families. In fact, they were two of the best friends I ever had and two of the most genuine kids I had ever met, yet for some reason, unknown to me, we were supposed to be enemies.

By asking myself the question of why I was supposed to hate my friends, I was able to finally grasp that hatred is something we learn. I began to understand that it comes from ignorance and it is a destructive force. I then thought about hatred and how it had entered into the life of Epi and his village. It was hatred that killed his mother, father and sister. It was hatred that left the old man and Epi alive to endure the traumatic memories. But was it also the hatred of the assailants that left them to live? Did they figure it was crueler to force an old man to live after he watched everything and everyone he ever loved die? Did they find it amusing that the youngest child in the village would have to fend for himself with no mother or father? Or was the hatred of the massacre so indiscriminate, so indifferent, that the attackers simply didn't care about the fate of the old man or Epi?

While these questions will never be answered and my understanding of how such hatred can infect a person to their soul is something I will never be able to fathom, my experience in getting to know Epi and George left me with the following thought: If hatred is something we learn, we can unlearn it, just like Epi, George and I did so many years ago. And the beautiful part is we did it without having to say a single word.

THE INCIDENT

The incident occurred in the summer of 1990, after the fall of the Berlin Wall. We had flown back to Berlin and were visiting our friends, Adelheid, Jurgen, Heike, George and Epi. This particular day we arrived at a park to have a picnic lunch and enjoy an outdoor sunny afternoon. Our group was walking on the sidewalk next to the entrance of a park when an old four door sedan drove by. As it passed there was a commotion with some shouting that startled us.

George and I were talking and looked up to see Frank with his two bad ankles, lamely hobbling after the car with his cane raised in the air while he was throwing F Bombs at its occupants. We watched as the sedan with four German youth sped away, hearing their laughter at the sight of Frank giving chase. It was the only time in my life I had ever seen Frank attempt to run. Out of breath, he slowly turned around and he walked back towards us. George and I wondered, what could have occurred to make him that angry? As we observed Frank, I saw his demeanor immediately shift from anger to concern.

I had been so caught up watching Frank and trying to understand what the youth in the sedan had done, that I failed to notice our mothers standing next to Epi. He was visibly shaking and tears were forming in his eyes. Near his feet there were shards from a glass bottle. Instantly, the gravity of the moment hit me. I understood why Frank was running.

I understood what the youth in the sedan had shouted. The look in Epi's eyes, the uncontrollable shaking of his body, and his tears were ingrained in my memory.

I watched as the adults surrounded him. The world went silent and my body was paralyzed. Seconds seemed to last for minutes. I was held captive as an observer to the events unfolding. Without sound or touch, the nuances of the scene were magnified. Everything I saw was burned into my memory, to become a wound that would eventually heal, but always leave a scar. The sedan had disappeared down the road, only to reappear in my thoughts along with the faces of the German youth, Frank running, and the fear in Epi.

After what I suppose was just a few moments, the intensity of the situation began to calm. My hearing returned, and I walked with George as our entire group slowly began to resume our way into the park, stepping over the shattered glass. Once inside the safety of the park, George and I finally had a chance to comfort Epi. However, we both were unsure of what to do or say. Together, we walked up to him and simply nodded to ask if he was okay. He nodded in return. After a few moments, the three of us looked up again and we smiled. We had come to the park as three friends to play, so we walked off together and did just that, while understanding that none of us would ever be quite the same.

Dezso

The first time I met Dezso (pronounced Deh sure) was January of 1988. The last time I saw him was June. Six months. That's it. We met in the Auslander School, two young children, foreigners to both Berlin and each other. He was the first of my classmates to come up to me and ask me my name. At the moment he introduced himself, I was terrified. I was alone and younger than the other kids who all came from the countries I had been taught to fear as an American child of the 1980's. I distinctly recall sitting alone at recess worried that a gang of them would come up to me, this wimpy American, to claim their own victory in the Cold War. I felt I was a sad representation of what Americans were supposed to be: tough, masculine, and confident. Dezso changed all this.

All the kids were looking at me. They didn't even try to hide it. I felt like an animal trapped in a zoo. As the seconds passed, the tension between us increased. It seemed as if the weight of the Cold War was bearing down right in the middle of this school and I was its epicenter. Nobody knew what to do. I was too afraid to make first contact, as I would later understand all of them were, too. As I glanced from group to group, country to country, I noticed Dezso right away. We were naturally drawn to each other.

Dezso was the closest in age to me, he being twelve to my ten. We had similar thin builds, shared a desperate need for braces, and had distinct noses from our lineages that would require our teenage years to grow into: his Hungarian, mine a Sicilian-Jew combo. The two of us made eye contact. He then turned to his older brother Tomas and his sister Katarina, whispered something to them while motioning toward me and suddenly began to lead the three of them across the courtyard. As they approached, I glanced around the perimeter and saw Russia, Poland, Czechoslovakia and Cuba anticipating this new turn of events. When Dezso and his Hungarian delegation arrived, he immediately extended his hand and repeated the few German words we had learned that morning.

"Ich heisse Dezso," he said while extending his hand.

I was still unsure what to do, my American wimpiness getting the better of me.

"Ich heisse Dezso," he repeated, and this time Tomas and Katarina stated their names.

In what at the time was the most courageous act of my life, I extended my hand and replied, "Ich heisse Eric." The three of us then shook hands and smiled at each other, in the process removing the thick tension that had blanketed the school since my arrival. Dezso's diplomacy allowed Russia, Poland, Czechoslovakia and Cuba to join us. What ensued was quite the scene, a dozen kids from a half-dozen countries and no common language, communicating through a third language of which we all knew approximately 4 sentences. But that was all it took, for the recess ball rang and we all walked back to the classroom as new acquaintances on our way to becoming friends. We all had a new motivation to learn German, too. The more German we could understand, the more we could communicate with each other.

Over the next few weeks, our collective ability to speak German grew exponentially, and in turn, we were all able to share more about our lives and our home countries. Dezso and I began to develop a close friendship, being that we were roughly the same age and technically the only non-teenagers in the group. With the power of words, German words, we discovered how, despite our backgrounds, we enjoyed many of the same things. We listened to the same music, enjoyed games such as chess, and creating complex designs with Legos. At times, our lack of a common language frustrated us when we had something important to say, but we managed. As our friendship solidified, Dezso invited me to go to his home after school. He explained that his parents wanted to meet me and make me a true Hungarian meal.

After getting the okay from my folks, I went with Dezso, Tomas and Katarina to their apartment, near Alexanderplatz. My mom and Frank decided not to attend, partly due to fear that Stazi were watching and their presence with Dezso's family could have unintended consequences for his family in Berlin or back in Budapest, and partly to allow me to experience this moment on my own, without them being a crutch on which I would rely. Their fears of the Stazi were only partly founded, for the fact that Dezso and I were foreign children, allowed us to play by a different set of rules than the adults. We had the freedom of association that the adults of East Berlin could only dream of.

I was nervous as the four us arrived at Dezso's home. I had always been taught that when someone extends an invitation to their home, it is a sign of respect and not to be taken lightly. I didn't want to disappoint Dezso or his parents. Furthermore, in my mind, I felt like I was in fact representing my home, the U.S. If I made a good impression on this Hungarian family, they would forever have a favorable opinion about Americans, and in turn tell all their friends and family back in Budapest how great Americans truly are. Conversely, if I messed up, I would single-handedly contribute another layer of ice in the Cold War. The pressure was one.

Dezso opened the front door announcing to his parents that we had arrived. The four of us stepped inside to an apartment full of the most magnificent smells. Due to the special occasion, his father and mother, also named Dezso and Katarina, had prepared a traditional meal of Hungarian Goulash with homemade stuffed dumplings. I vividly recall the aroma of the goulash and dumplings that permeated my olfactory senses mixed with the scents of paprika, slowly cooked brisket, and a pallet full of other spices. I couldn't wait for supper.

Upon our arrival, Dezso's parents welcomed me with sincere smiles full of warmth and appreciation. In the best German they could manage, they asked me some of the same questions Dezso and I had asked each other weeks ago in the courtyard of the school. At times, they would ask Dezso a question in Hungarian which he would then translate in to German. He would then translate my response back into Hungarian. It was a slow conversation, but the complexity of it was not lost on me at the time. As I listened to their family speak Hungarian, I had to keep reminding myself that I was not in some dream, that this was in fact my life, and I was actually without my mom and Frank, in the apartment of a Hungarian family, in Berlin, with German as our common language. There was no way I could ever explain this to any of my friends back home.

Soon after, we were sitting around the table enjoying our feast, communicating as best as we could. When our German broke down, we used smiles and charade hand gestures to convey our messages. As this remarkable meal progressed, I understood with more clarity that his family was not only offering me food, they were asking me to accept their family and their culture. The fact that I was an American made their offer all the more significant. By accepting their offer, without hesitation, I had passed the test and truly was an ambassador for my country and as a reward, had one of the most spectacular meals of my life, consisting of goulash, dumplings and most important of all, a friendship that will always be with me.

TRABBI

A Mercedes Benz you're not
A true people's car
With a fiberglass cardboard foundation

Your size is lacking
But character is not
For no car will ever compare

To a lawnmower engine
Two horses of power
Spitting ugly exhaust from your tail

You demand precision at any speed
No errors of inattention
Or you and your cargo will meet your makers

The wait to possess you
Is sixteen years
A disappointment you will never be

Conceived in the East
A joke in the West
A necessity in the Middle

The mobility of freedom
Is all you have to offer
Yes, a Mercedes Benz you're not

PLACES

SCHOOL

There were two options for my schooling, neither of which was very appealing to me. The first alternative that was recommended by our American friends and the U.S. Embassy was to have me attend an American school on the military base in West Berlin. This would have required a 2 hour trip to and from school, including crossing the border every day. In addition, my mom would have had to go with me each day and stay in West Berlin the entire time.

The length of the trip and the constant crossing of the border was only one concern that factored into us not choosing this alternative. My parents wanted me to experience the culture of another country and learn the language. I wasn't going to get that by attending an American school in West Berlin. It would have defeated one of the major advantages of living in a foreign country, especially one as socially and politically different as East Germany. So, against the advice of the embassy and our American friends, my parents enrolled me in an East German school for foreigners.

The premise of the school for foreigners, auslanders in German, was very basic. All non-German children living in Berlin were enrolled in a class for six months where they studied nothing but German. At the end of six months they would be placed into a regular German classroom, regardless of their fluency. It was truly a system of sink or swim. Although

I would not be in Berlin long enough for me to transfer to a German classroom, my experience with the East German education system and the placement of non-German speaking students into an intensive fluency program turned out to be one of the most transformative experience of my life.

The week before my classes began, my mom, Frank and I met the principal. Over the years I have forgotten his name so I now refer to him as Herr Schmidt. Herr Schmidt was a middle age man with thick glasses and he protruded a strong commitment to discipline and order. He spoke fluent English, but with the standard harsh sounding German accent. From the moment I met him he scared the crap out of me, which was his intent. He was not there to be my friend or build my esteem. It was his one and only job to make sure that in six months I spoke German. However, it wasn't only me, it was the dozen other kids in the class as well, each of whom spoke different languages. If he didn't have discipline and order, he would fail at his job which meant he would fail all of us.

We met Herr Schmidt at the school which began with a tour of the small facility and he informing us that today was to be the only day a member of the faculty would speak English to me. Starting next week I could only communicate in German. I remember asking myself how the hell was I going to do that when I knew exactly three words, with one of them being Sheisse, which I silently repeated to myself.

As he gave us the tour of the classrooms and small playground area he informed us what we could expect of the school and what the school expected of us. In a matter of fact tone he told my folks it was their responsibility as parents to speak German at home and if they didn't know it, they must learn it! My mom knew even less than I did and Frank was going off memories of German class from the early 1960's.

We continued the conversation as we walked into his office where we sat down at his desk. He went on to explain that there were only three items I was allowed to bring with me to school: sharpened pencils with erasers, a German English Dictionary and lunch. Nothing else was to be permitted, because anything more would be a distraction and distractions would inhibit me from learning German. As he explained, again, I was in school to learn German: nothing more, nothing less. If I obeyed his instructions, I would be fluent by June.

Herr Schmidt's extreme confidence that he could teach me German was on the order of arrogance. In response to his statement, my mom asked, "But Herr Schmidt, what happens if my son doesn't learn German?" There was a long pause as Herr Schmidt looked at me, then my mom, then Frank. He returned his eyes to my mom and looking squarely in her eyes, in his heavy German accent, "Mrs. McConnell, you do not understand. Your son WILL learn German." With that, our orientation was over. He politely walked us to the door and said he looked forward to seeing me in class next week.

First Day of School

Thinking back to the first day of Junior High, I can still recall the sights and sounds associated with perhaps the most traumatic day of childhood. I distinctly remember the anxiety and nervousness of that first day, that first hour, that first minute, that very first moment when I understood that I was not a kid anymore. I longed for the safety of my sixth grade classroom and the security of the friends I had known my entire life. And as I made my way to my first class, my mind was running amok, recalling everything I had ever heard about Jr. High. None of it was reassuring. I prayed I wouldn't get my ass kicked and that nothing embarrassing would happen over the course of the next 7 hours. For in Jr. High, especially on that first day, you would rather die than be embarrassed.

Unfortunately, I had to experience this awful first day of Jr. High not once, but twice. The first time was my first day at the Auslander school. However, on this occasion I was only ten years old, couldn't speak the language, and I didn't know a single other kid. But it got worse.

Upon entering the school I discovered that all the other kids were actually teenagers, most of them 14-17 years old with just a couple of 12 year olds. To my horror, all the other kids were from the list of notorious countries I had been taught to both hate and fear growing up in 1980's America. But it got worse.

35

The rumor machine was in full effect, because before I set one foot on the campus, they all heard I was coming and were anticipating my arrival. There was absolutely zero chance to find security in the anonymity of being a wallflower. Whether I wanted it or not, I was the center of attention. And this was just the first minute, of the first hour, of the first day of my enrollment in the Auslander Schule.

On that first morning, my mom had made the 45 minute trip into the center of Berlin with me. She promised me that she would go with me the first week, but after that she assured me that I would be comfortable enough to make the trek on my own. When we arrived at the school she knew I was upset and asked me if I wanted her to walk with me to my classroom. Internally I wanted nothing more, but I responded by telling her I was okay and could do it. I figured the only thing worse than being the target of my enemies would be if I was also known as a mamma's boy. So, as bravely as I could, I gave her a hug and told her I would see her in few hours when class was out. I turned and walked up the steps to the school, looked back once and saw my mom watching me. It wasn't until I became a parent myself that I understood the look in her eyes as she watched me disappear into the school grounds.

I reluctantly walked up the steps and purposefully delayed finding my way to my classroom. When I finally arrived my heart was pounding. I took a deep breath and walked into the room to see Herr Schmidt and all the other kids staring at me. The silence was unbearable and the nefarious intentions of the other kids were barely masked by their matter of fact faces. I was positive at that specific moment in time that the next six months were going to be torture, via express delivery from Russia, Poland, Hungry, Czechoslovakia and Cuba. I had never been so terrified in my life. Acting on instinct alone, I quickly found the empty seat which of course had been left in front just for me. As I sat down, my back to the rest of the class, I could feel the collective power of the group observing me and the satisfaction that their plan to place me up front had been executed to perfection. Moments later the bell rang and all thoughts in the room turned to German, and, of course, the countdown to recess.

We had fifteen minutes to spend in the courtyard. When the bell rang, I pretended to fumble through my backpack as if I was searching for an item of great importance. The room emptied out and it was just me and Herr Schmidt. True to his word, without speaking English, he ordered me in German to go out to the playground with the other kids. Even though I couldn't understand a single word he said, he made himself distinctly understood. I knew protesting wouldn't accomplish much, so I followed orders and walked myself to the courtyard.

When I arrived I discovered that the other kids had split up into their respective countries and they were all talking in their native tongues. This momentary break from speaking Deutsche was allowed, at least early on. Even in the respite from the rules, the other kids had an advantage over me, for all of them, with the exception of the boy from Cuba, had at least one other person with whom to speak. I, on the other hand, was forced to remain silent and alone and listen to the hodgepodge of Eastern European languages fill the air. While they were occupied with the chance to speak in their native tongues, I took the opportunity to slide into a corner where I could sit down and have a snack. I was finally the wallflower I longed to be.

My time in anonymity was progressing without incident until there was about five minutes left for recess. It was then that I noticed I was noticed. The other kids, still divided into their own countries and talking to each other within their groups, somehow managed to make a unison effort to look at me, even the boy from Cuba. And that's when it happened, the Hungarians decided to make their move.

There were three of them, Tomas, Katarina and Dezso, who were siblings. The three of them slowly walked my direction while the other countries stayed on the sidelines, waiting and watching. My heart began to race and my body filled with adrenaline. I wanted to run, but knew I had nowhere to escape. Besides, being a wimpy kid, I already knew from experience that running only makes it worse. It is always better to take my licks and get it over with. So, I stood up, putting on the best front I could as the Hungarians approached.

The oldest Tomas, was 17, followed by Katarina who was 15 and Dezso, who was 12. I knew they were from Hungary because one of the first German lessons of the day was that we all had to tell each other our names and the country we were from. Having to tell these communist kids I was from the U.S.A and specifically California only added fuel to their fire, or so I imagined. Now that we were outside, with no teachers around, I found myself surrounded by the siblings from Budapest. As I quickly glanced around the courtyard I observed that all eyes were now on the four us and there was no more speaking in native tongues. The tension was thick. We all knew that one false move by either side could begin our own Cold War in the middle of the Auslander School. There was an extended silence as the Hungarians and I tried to determine what the next move would be. And then three words were spoken that would forever change my life.

"Ich heisse Dezso," he said while extending his hand.

I was confused and unable to reply.

"Ich heisse Dezso," he repeated.

"Ich heisse Eric," I finally replied while accepting the handshake.

Then Tomas, Katarina, Dezo and I introduced ourselves to each other, using the few sentences of German we had learned that morning. Could this really be happening I asked myself in disbelieve? These kids didn't want to gang up on me? They wanted to become friends? How was it possible that just a week ago I was in Southern California, but today I found myself talking in German and shaking hands with Hungarians in the middle of East Berlin?

My whole world came crashing down. Everything I was sure I knew was now upheaved. As the four of us got to know each other, all the other kids came over and the handshakes and speaking in German continued as we learned each other's names and where we were from. Unlike in the classroom, this time it was different. This time it was genuine and the start of something larger. It was a miraculous moment! We were a dozen kids who spoke half a dozen languages and now found ourselves conversing in a language none of us knew. In the process we tossed aside the politics of our fathers and grandfathers and did what was natural, we became friends.

The friendships strengthened over the ensuing months as our collective ability to speak German improved. In fact, the power of our friendships was so important to us that it became the single greatest motivation for us to learn as much German as possible so that we could communicate more effectively with one another. We all had so much we wanted to share with each other.

The shift from enemies to friends was all made possible from that moment when Dezso found the courage to say those three words and extend his hand. His courage gave me my own courage to return the gesture. We overcame our fear of each other, ended the isolation of the courtyard, and in our own small way, helped bring the world one step closer to tearing down the Wall.

LOST IN EAST BERLIN

The conductor's voice came over the loud speakers of the U-Bahn. My German wasn't good enough to understand most of what he said, so I just sat there hoping that whatever it was didn't affect me and the train would get on its way. When he had finished, everyone on board began to exit. I began to panic, for this was a station I had never visited. Perhaps, there is something wrong with train I thought and a new one would come along. So I did the only thing I could, I followed the mass of people as they exited the train, and much to my dismay, the station itself.

While following the masses, I quickly pieced together what was happening. There was a problem with the tracks, not the train. In response, there were streetcars ready to take us around the broken tracks and eventually reconnect us with the U-Bahn. A sense of relief came over me as I planned for the few minute detour from my designated route. Although I didn't know the streetcar system, I figured I would do what I had just done with the train; I would follow the crowd back to the U-Bahn. Surely I reasoned, if they had all unexpectedly exited together they would all rejoin the train together.

I found myself on the streetcar traveling through a section of East Berlin I had never visited. I kept looking for a familiar landmark, but the more I searched, the more disoriented I became. The first stop came and only a few people exited. This couldn't be it. So I made the quick decision to wait for the next stop. A few minutes later the same scenario played out; the streetcar stopped, only a few people exited, and I, waiting for the mass exodus, stayed put. This scenario played itself out a few more times with the mass exodus never occurring. Eventually the streetcar, which was now just me in the back and an old hausfrau in the front, came to its final stop. The woman exited leaving just me. I was paralyzed with fear and refused to exit. For the streetcar was my life-line. It was all I knew. Without it, I was going to drown. The conductor yelled some German words (doesn't German always sound like yelling when you don't understand it), which I knew to mean that this was my last stop, whether I wanted to get off or not.

I stepped onto the cobblestone street then watched as the streetcar sped off, leaving me alone. It was a sinking feeling to see my only way home abandon me. I couldn't make a call because there were no phones and besides, I had no idea where I was, so it wasn't like my mom or Frank could come and get me. To make matters worse, it was late afternoon and the elongated shadows of the buildings told me that nighttime was approaching. The only thing worse than being lost in a foreign city, is being lost in a foreign city at night. My unfortunate predicament overwhelmed me and suddenly I began to cry.

As I shed my first few tears an unexpected voice called out to me, "Crying isn't going to solve your problem," he said. It was my own voice and it came from a part of me that I never knew existed, one that was filled with courage and resourcefulness. It was a part of me that had waited my entire life for this moment and was now ready to seize the opportunity to prove to me he existed. With the promise that he would get us home, he then took command of our sinking ship.

I lifted my head and immediately stopped crying. After a few deep breaths to center myself, I looked around to assess my situation. I was at an unfamiliar four way intersection with street names I had never encountered. East and west meant nothing to me, because the streetcar had taken me through the maze of endless city streets before dropping me off somewhere in the middle (or was it the end) of the labyrinth. I scanned my surroundings to see if there were any people in the immediate vicinity I could turn to for help. To my disappointment it was just me. If I was going to make it home, I was going have to do it alone.

I paused to think. I told myself there had to be something I recognized that would point me in the right direction. I revisited the buildings and street names, hoping they would jog a memory. There was no such luck. After what seemed like an eternity, I was about to give up. So much for the courageous and resourceful me I thought. But then, on a last whim, a Hail Mary of sorts, I looked up. A smile came over me, for I found my solution.

Off in the distance, towering above the buildings around me, I saw the iconic Fernsehturm, Berlin's equivalent of the Seattle Space Needle. That was the center of town, at Alexanderplatz, which was the major transportation hub of the city. I had been there many times with my mom and Frank and knew if I could get there, I was home free, literally. So with a rejuvenated spirit, I quickly used my long legs to traverse what turned out to be about three miles, never losing sight of the tower. With each step, it grew larger and my confidence grew accordingly. Finally, as I arrived in Alexanderplatz a barrage of memories hit me. I knew where I was! I knew the hamburger stand and the pickle cart were just around the corner to be followed by the U-Bahn station. My detour was over and I was back to my original route.

About a half-hour later, I exited the S-Bahn in Marzahn and began the final walk to our apartment. Almost immediately I saw my mom who was out searching for me. Frank had stayed home on the chance that I returned while my mom was out looking for me. We ran up to each other and embraced in a tight hug. I was finally home. As we walked together to our apartment, I explained all the events that had happened and how I managed to find my way home by looking up at the Fernsehturm. This out of ordinary trip introduced me to myself and became one of the most important detours of my life.

A Supermarket in East Berlin

Move over Allen Ginsberg
This ain't your supermarket
No avocado wives or aisles of husbands in this joint
Just little old hausfraus
Carefully navigating the coal dust coated floors
To pick from the half empty shelves of their half empty lives
Always wanting more,
More lettuce, more tomatoes, more grapes and bananas
Oh, for a single banana in February
No more schnitzel, potatoes or cabbage Mr. Czar
Please send me an apple of hope today
For the terror of aisle 1 has engulfed me
Where the bibulous men buy bottles of Berliner Pilsner,
Iron Curtain style
As they choke on their unfiltered *Karo* Cancer Sticks
And laugh at the Marlborough Man

Wait, there's a commotion in the back
It's the sounds of life
One single cart full of magical gherkins
A rush of madness for this edible green in a world drowning in black and white
The yellow and blue is within my grasp
She shoves me
The old haus frau
Our eyes lock
"Mein!"

I step aside
At 4 foot 11
The posture of two World Wars weighs on her shoulders
The Russian Retribution wrinkles her skin
The Arthritis of Allied Abandonment attacks her joints
She has earned the contents of the cart
And perhaps someday
A banana in February

A SUPERMARKET IN WEST BERLIN

Sausages! Sausages! There's a whole floor of Sausages!
Bratwursts, breakfast links, Spanish and Italian
A smorgasbord of finely cased meats
Ripening my salivating taste buds
This is just the sixth floor!
So many more to explore
Fruits and vegetables
Breads and cheeses
Beer and Wine
With names I can't pronounce
From countries I've never heard of
All in front of me
My olfactory overloaded
Teasing my ever hungry stomach
With the smells of endlessly impossible culinary delights
Each floor a journey of discovery
It's a world of endlessly edible possibilities
Telling the story of human history
All of it,
Under one roof
Thousands of years of scientific achievements
Centuries of political upheaval
The rich past making a full present
Full of infinite choices
Finally answering the most important question of all
What shall I have for dinner tonight?

THE WALL

VIEWS OF THE WALL

Throughout our journey we developed an intimate relationship with the Wall. It became a part of us, our identity. While the Wall was the iconic global symbol of the divide between East and West and all that each represented, it was also, in a strange way, a unifying presence. For it brought people together through shared common experience and united purpose, its destruction. In doing so, it shaped the three of us and our relationships with those we met, which was highlighted by our unique circumstance of living simultaneously on both sides while not fully being a part of either. As I contemplated how to recall my experiences and the seemingly contradictory reality of the Wall, it dawned on me that it was not contradictory at all. For its reality changed depending on the perspective. And, through these different perspectives, the whole of the Wall became much more complex than the traditional narrative of East vs. West or Good vs. Evil. To attempt to capture these different perspectives and the whole reality of the Wall, I wrote the following six narratives, each from different physical experiences of mine, which took place to the east, west, above, below and in the middle of the Wall.

The sixth and final narrative ties these experiences together through the retelling of an ethical dilemma our family faced. The story was originally written as an assignment for an Ethics class I took in Grad school. I have included an edited version of that essay.

VIEW FROM THE EAST

One morning, my class went on a fieldtrip to tour the city center. We walked down Unter den Linden until we came to the metal barricade which marked the end of our journey. Unter den Linden was the main east-west street in Berlin which was bisected by the Wall. It is in the heart of historic Berlin and included many notable landmarks, including the iconic Brandenburg Gate. It was here, in the center and most visible part of Berlin, where the implications of the Wall were perhaps greatest. For the Brandenburg Gate and other cultural relics of Berlin's proud past were off limits, *verboten*. They were highly visible and heavily guarded in their special place located right in the center of No Man's Land. It was as if the Brandenburg Gate and its environs were timeless temples of the gods and we humans, from both the east and the west, were prohibited from entering their sanctuary. In our collective exile, we were reminded that the gods were here before the Wall and they would be here long after. The Wall was our fate, the people of this time who lived it and breathed it.

My classmates and I spread out in line at the three foot metal gate, looking at the sights before us, prohibited from taking one more step west. But Unter den Linden itself kept going right into the Wall itself. It traversed through No Man's Land, under the Wall and then became an inhabited street once again in the West. Its path included the Brandenburg Gate which stood in all its majestic glory, a relic from the past, untouched by human hands for more than a quarter century, except for the East German guards. It was the one place that made me an equal to my classmates, for, like them, it was a place I could never visit, unlike the other side of the Wall.

As we silently observed the scene before us, we spotted people waving in the distance. They were atop bleachers that were erected on the west side of the Wall along the same bisected street we now stood. The bleachers allowed West Berliners and tourists to view Brandenburg Plaza and the city behind the Wall, which at this very moment in time included us. The anonymous people on the other end kept waving, expecting us to reciprocate. Instead they received blank stares.

It was at this moment, that I fully understood the fate of my friends. They could never see Berlin from the vantage point of the anonymous people across the way. They were forever stuck in the city behind us, forced only to dream of the city in front of us, the city they could see, the city they could hear, the city they could smell, the city where they could even communicate with its people through a simple wave. It was then that I determined this spot, the most historic in all of Berlin, both East and West, was in fact the cruelest of all.

View from West

There is an old Twilight Zone episode titled, "People Are Alike All Over", in which two astronauts crash land on Mars. The lone survivor meets a race of friendly Martians who happen to be human beings. As the story unfolds, the Martians bring him to their city where they have constructed a typical mid-century apartment that would be found on Earth. When the man is left alone to rest, he explores the apartment and everything is first-rate, even the scotch. But, as time progresses he finds that it is an apartment with no windows, just walls. He begins to frantically search for a way out. In a panic, he rushes to the front door and opens it, only to find there is no outside and there is no apartment, just walls. Suddenly, the walls fall down. He then realizes that he is an animal, caged in a Martian zoo exhibit called "Earthling in his Native Habitat." With the walls now down, he looks out to see Martian families observing him, fascinated by his behavior. He screams, imploring that he is not an animal. He is a man and men are supposed to be free. But his begging is to no avail, and he is forced to permanently reside behind the lone remaining wall.

I think of this episode when I recollect the day my mom, Frank and I decided to go to West Berlin to tour the Wall. We had been to the West on a few occasions, having seen and touched the Wall, but we were always visiting for some other reason and the Wall was an afterthought. This trip, however, was all about the Wall. It was the day the picture of me that is now the cover of this memoir was taken.

For our adventure we chose to visit the area around Unter den Linden and the Brandenburg Gate. Since this was the center of the city, it was the most heavily visited area of the Wall and subsequently had the most diverse collection of Wall art. Whereas the East side of the Wall was a stark white behemoth of concrete where no person could walk, the West side was open and free. It was a chance for any and all people who visited to touch it and use their artistic ingenuity to defile it with nonviolent protest against the government that built it. Nowhere else in the world was there such a stark contrast on the regulation of human behavior found in such a small setting.

As we walked along the Wall taking pictures of our favorite art, we came upon the bleachers along Unter den Linden and Brandenburg Gate. They had been installed in order to provide the West with a view of the East and the Gate itself, since the Wall was tall enough to block all views of this historic plaza. As we approached the steps of the bleachers I hesitated. I recalled the view from the East experienced just a couple weeks prior. I was conflicted about going where my friends, specifically Dezso, could not, and especially this place, for now it would be me looking across at them.

Reluctantly, I climbed the steps to the top of the bleachers and eventually saw the East, which by this time I knew so well. I could see where I had walked many times with Mom and Frank. I observed the people, the cars and the buses moving in their everyday life. It was, and still is, incomprehensible to me, how at this spot, I was standing on the border between two worlds. One was similar to the world I knew back home, the other, on full display in front of me, was an artificial world full of secrets and mysteries. It was the other side of Narnia's wardrobe.

As I took in the sights in front of me, I was purposefully looking for the metal gate my class had visited. Finally spotting it, I closed my eyes to recall that moment from a few weeks ago. At once, I became both the animal in the zoo and the observing family. I was trapped like Dezso and the others, yet I was free like the strangers who had waved to us. I opened my eyes and saw people at the same spot I had been, people who were now staring back at me. I had to make a quick decision, should I wave?

When I had been on the East I was angry at the strangers for waving. But, from the vantage point of the bleachers in the West it became clear to me that I had to wave. Waving meant I recognized their plight and their humanity. A simple wave was the one means we had to communicate and overcome the power of the Wall. By waving, I realized I wasn't demeaning them, but rather I was refusing to let them be caged, and in the process, preventing them from the fate of the astronaut in the Martian zoo.

View from the Top

One afternoon we met some friends for lunch. They decided it would be fun for us to see the bird's eye view of Berlin. We found ourselves in the restaurant perched in the center ball of the Fernsehturm, the iconic television tower which is Berlin's version of the Seattle Space Needle. It is located in Alexanderplatz in the center of Berlin and consists of a long slender base with a large ball hundreds of feet up that allows for panoramic vistas of Berlin and its surrounding environs.

After we arrived at the restaurant, we were seated at our table, which, to our surprise, was moving slowly in a circle. It turned out the entire restaurant was built on a moving axis and was designed to make a full rotation around Berlin in an hour. While I can only imagine what the view must be like today, at the time it afforded the opportunity to see the two Berlins from the perspective of the clouds.

As the hour counted down, the scene of daily life below unfolded before us. From my window seat vantage point I noticed immediately stark contrasts between East and West. The buildings and the streets of the East seemed old and crumbling when viewed in the same panoramic setting as its modern western brother. The pace of traffic was much slower in the East. It was as if the people of the East were moving, but had no real destination, whereas the pace in the West was more hurried, frantic, with everyone having somewhere to be other than where they were.

It really was two distinct and separate worlds, or more accurately, one world with an island in its middle.

The notion of West Berlin as an island was perplexing to me. I had always thought of the East as the island, and the West with its freedoms as the bedrock. But from the vantage point of Fernsehturm it was evident that the freedom of West Berlin was actually restricted. While those in the East could travel as far as my eyes could see, those in the West could only travel to the Wall. The Wall served the dual purpose of keeping those in the East out, and those in the West in. This was a subtle change in my understanding of Berlin, but significant in my still developing notion of what freedom really means.

As the hour concluded, I reflected on this brief but significant journey that ended right where it started. A sense of sadness lingered, for I saw how magnificent Berlin, the whole, one city not two, truly was. But the Wall and the ghosts of history's greatest villains had destroyed it. My final glance was of the Wall and No Man's Land and the divide it created. I wondered if the Wall would ever come down, and if it did, whether the two halves could once again become whole. Both seemed like impossible tasks.

View from Below

Ghosts exist all around us, silently hidden in plain view for all see, but it is up to us, the living, to find them. I began searching for them immediately upon our arrival in Berlin. It was during our excursions to West Berlin, when traveling between the Wall, where I discovered many of Berlin's most prominent ghosts resided. They lived underground, directly beneath No Man's Land, in the abandoned U-Bahn stations that were technically in the East, but located along the tracks to the West.

I distinctly recall one of our initial encounters with the underground ghosts. My mom and I were traveling to West Berlin through the Friedrichstrasse crossing. We rode the S-Bahn from our apartment in Marzahn to the end of the line at Friedrichstrasse. Upon exiting I observed many platforms, each designated for its specific train that would eventually disperse the East Berliners to their destinations throughout the city. On the far end there was a final platform that was fenced off from view. I could hear the trains coming and going, and when the sun cooperated, if I looked very carefully between the soft green fabric walls that divided east from west, I could make out the shadows of the people on the other side. The East Berliners seemed to ignore this last platform, block it from their minds as if it didn't exist. But for me, it was real, and unlike the people around me, I had been there. I had been a shadow.

To get to this platform, we had to cross the highly secured border underneath Friedrichstrasse station, which depending on the lines, could take anywhere from thirty minutes to nearly two hours. On this particular morning, the line moved quickly and when the final border agent stamped our passports, we were free to go back above ground to the platform on the other side, to the land of shadows. It was an awkward feeling, being in a place where I was literally meters away from where I had just been, yet the train I was about to catch would take me to a destination those on the other side could never go.

We boarded the train and began our ten minute voyage that started above the streets of East Berlin and would conclude in the West, on the other side of the Wall. As the train headed for West Berlin, it had to initially travel above the streets of the East before crossing into No Man's Land, which forced it underground. It was here, underneath the streets of East Berlin and No Man's Land, where the ghosts resided.

They emerged suddenly out of the darkness of the tunnel. Their home was the abandoned metro stations in the heart of East Berlin that could be seen only by people on the trains headed for the West. Nobody spoke as our train slowly passed the stations. We were fearful of waking its inhabitants. In unison with the strangers on the train, we communally observed their lair. It was covered in decades old dust, the stairs boarded up, the newspaper racks empty and no trace of civilians to be found. The only signs of life were the accusing eyes of East German guards, seated in what were once ticket booths, fixating on the train as it passed their domain.

My mom and I called these metro stops "ghost stations". When we would pass one I would purposefully refrain from blinking so I could capture ever detail in front of me. Doing so helped me imagine the people in rush hour, decades before, filling the stations, hustling on and off our very train, part of a single Berlin. I pictured how grand it must have been for these stations to be full of people, at times ordinary civilians, at other times soldiers in war, waiting for the trains to take them wherever they needed or desired to go. How marvelous it must have been for those Berliners of the distant past to have lived in a single Berlin, to have the freedom to use the very stations in front of me while blissfully unaware of the future fate that awaited Berlin, or their own fate, which permanently captured them underground, where they would haunt the Berliners of the present for nearly thirty years.

When the ghost stations receded back into the darkness and our train eventually arrived in the sunlight of West Berlin, I took a moment to comprehend what I just experienced. Through visiting Berlin's ghosts in their underground lair, I learned an essential truth about ghosts. They are memories of the past that haunt the present and influence the future. Fortunately now, a quarter century later, the Friedrichstrasse walls are down, the ghost stations are no longer *verboten*, and a unified Berlin has new ghosts to find, if you just know where to look.

VIEW FROM THE MIDDLE

When we crossed through Checkpoint Charlie we were literally walking right through the middle of No Man's Land. It was a journey that took us outside the constructed boundaries of civilization. Charlie was the place where the two titans of civilization were separated by only a few meters and the rules that governed life ceased to exist; they were replaced by an existence that had no past or future, only the present. It was a present with one specific aim – to find a way out.

To access Charlie from the East we had to walk down a quiet street. It was almost an afterthought, a street so well hidden that you wouldn't know how to get there unless you had been there before and nobody would dare give you directions. Although it always seemed deserted, we knew that the moment we stepped on this street we were being watched, for nobody walked or drove this street by accident.

We would enter Charlie with the following rules: stay quiet and speak only if spoken to. We would then silently shuffle through security, literally walking through No Man's Land with its hidden eyes recording our every step. It was an eerie feeling standing in a place with people you couldn't see watching you while they were silently making their presence known. Worse, it was terrifying to know these invisible people could literally make you disappear if they determined you didn't have the correct papers. I always had a fear that the guards wouldn't believe who I was, that they would make some erroneous conclusion that my mom and Frank were smuggling East German children to the West and I would disappear. It was a fear that only subsided when I left the limbo that was Charlie and took my first step on sacred western ground.

Eventually, we would make it to the other side which was a stark contrast to the East. We would exit the strict security of the land between two worlds to enter a busy metropolitan street. The energy of the West always took a moment to adjust, for it hit us all at once. It was an area filled with noise and life. It was a world full of color. People were moving about, cars going to and fro, construction projects adding new buildings and businesses within a stone's throw of the Wall. It was if the West had embraced this section and recognized it as a welcome point for those exiting the darkness.

Our journey through the middle always left us unprepared for when we entered our new world, whether it was the cold isolation of the East where we knew we were being watched or the hustling life of the West where we weren't even important enough to be noticed. Charlie was symbolic of our entire experience in Berlin; we were stranded in the middle between two distinct worlds, never fully a part of each. We were lost in Berlin, at Checkpoint Charlie, the center of it all.

An Ethical Dilemma

We were invited to dinner at the home of the Wedels, an East German family who had befriended us during our time in Berlin. They were a family of four: Jurgen, his wife Adelheide, and their two children, Ulrike and George. Ulrike was high-school age and George was about 9 years old, two years younger than I was at the time. Over our six months in Berlin, they became our closest friends and on this occasion had welcomed us to their home where they cooked an authentic East German meal.

The Wedels lived on the fourth floor of a turn of the century apartment that lacked an elevator. It was located about ten minutes from the center of Berlin and was situated on a cobblestone street that was the last avenue in the neighborhood ending at the Wall. Their proximity to the Wall and the power it possessed over our friends was remarkable. When we entered their home and looked out their fourth floor living room window we were greeted with a spectacular yet perplexing view. Since they were living on the last street before the Wall they had an unobstructed view of No Man's Land and the horizon beyond, which was filled with the sights of West Berlin. From the vantage point of their living room, the first thing they would see in the morning and last thing they would see at night before closing their curtains was a city they could never visit and of a freedom they could never experience.

I gazed out the window and fixated my eyes on the guard towers of No Man's Land. From this vantage point I observed an interesting fact about the Berlin Wall. There were actually two walls. On the East side there was a 12 foot concrete wall to mark the beginning of No Man's Land. From the Wedels' home it was just a couple of football fields away. On the other side of this first wall was the infamous No Man's Land, which was devoid of all human activity expect for the watchful eye of East German military stationed within the strategically placed guard towers. On the far end of No Man's Land was the iconic Berlin Wall itself, a monstrous structure of concrete that was a final reminder to the Wedels and all East Germans of their confinement.

After overcoming the shock of recognizing two walls and guard towers that were ordered to shoot on sight if needed, I gazed farther on to West Berlin in the distance. It took up the remainder of the visible horizon and was spectacular with its mix of urban forests and big city lights that began to take over with the onset of dusk. It seemed so close that I felt as if I could reach out and grab it while I concurrently heard its Western culture. It was at this moment, captured in the awe of West Berlin while standing in the East, that I understood what it was like to be an East Berliner. Our friends could never experience the foreign city they saw on a daily basis, the city that was literally a stone's throw away, the same city I had visited many times in our few months in East Berlin. It was a place that represented everything I had back in California.

In a very real sense, the view from their apartment was like gazing at heaven from just outside its gates while stuck in the land of limbo, for that was what East Berlin was, limbo. It wasn't hell, it wasn't heaven. It was just a place where you were stuck both physically and intellectually with the unfortunate circumstance of having your salvation displayed before your very eyes like a tormenting desert mirage that would never quench your thirst. It was here, with the visible background of the Wall and West Berlin that our ethical dilemma began.

During the course of dinner the conversation turned to the West as it always did with any East German we met. They were obsessed with the West, and in particular America and the three of us. In most cases, we were the first Americans they had ever met who weren't affiliated with the communist party in some way. Usually East Germans were surprised to discover that Americans were actually very similar to them in many ways. We were not anything like their preconception of us, which was based upon the exuberant lifestyles of the weekly soaps *Dallas* and *Dynasty*, which they viewed thanks to transmissions from West Berlin. On this particular night, the issue of the Rolling Stones came up. In just a few weeks, it was rumored that the Stones were going to be in West Berlin at the Brandenburg Gate to play a concert. It was not uncommon for well-known rock bands of the time to play concerts at the Wall and blast the speakers into the East as a form of protest. When I learned this, I pictured Neil Young and Springsteen at the Brandenburg Gate singing "Keep on Rockin in the Free World" and "Born in the USA".

The conversation became more animated with the insertion of the Stones, and before we knew it, Jurgen proclaimed that we should go see them. This seemed rather odd to us at first, since it was understood that they couldn't go. This sudden turn in the conversation also put us in an uncomfortable situation, since it highlighted the fact that there was an inequality between our family and theirs. Yet, Jurgen insisted in planning for us to see the Stones. It turned out the "we" he was talking about included him.

To this day, I am not exactly sure how Jurgen had the ability to travel to West Berlin, but the fact was that he was able to do so. The revelation that he could go to the concert with us changed the dynamic of the conversation. Initially, in Jurgen's enthusiasm he gave the impression that his family would be able to attend as well. For the next few minutes we discussed plans for the great pilgrimage to see the Stones at the Wall. The planning stopped when we noticed the silence and deflated look on the faces of Adelheid, Ulrike and George. Frank paused, then asked the obvious question of whether or not they could in fact go. The answer was a simple no. Only Jurgen would be going with us.

The response by Frank and my mom over the course of the next few minutes changed my understanding of what it means to be an ethical person and how one must evaluate quickly when confronted with such dilemmas. Upon learning that only Jurgen could go, we had two options; we could either continue on as planned or refuse to go. For Frank and my mom the answer was obvious. Without hesitation Frank told Jurgen that the three of us refused to go if Adelheid, Ulrike and George could not.

In terms of the ethical dilemma that presented itself, I have always broken it down into a simple question: Just because a person can do something, should they? The Stones dilemma also brought up the larger issue of our crossing the wall at any time. If we decided not to go to see the Stones on principle, then should we refrain from going at other times? The principle here wasn't just going to see the Stones, it was the very nature of going where others could not go. This one situation forced us to re-evaluate our own actions. From that moment in time forward, simply crossing the Wall for any reason became an ethical dilemma. On principle alone, we could never cross.

We eventually came to different conclusions on how to handle this new reality. For the remaining three months we were in East Berlin, Frank simply refused to go to West Berlin unless there was an absolute necessity. My mom and I decided to go less frequently. When we did, we modified the purpose for our trips by bringing back goods for our East German friends that were unavailable to them which also wouldn't be confiscated by the guards at the border crossing.

The unexpected outcome of our decision not to see the Stones was that we gained a level of respect from Adelheid, Ulrike, George and even Jurgen. It was perhaps the moment that solidified our friendship and built the trust that enabled us to remain close through the turmoil that came with the fall of the Wall, the collapse of the Soviet Union, and perhaps the most difficult of all, the simple passage of time. In addition, when Frank recounted this story to his East German class, he gained a level of respect that could only be earned through acting ethically. His students were literally shocked that he made that decision as it demonstrated a commitment to them and an understanding of their plight.

The fact was that due to elements out of our control, we were not equals with the East Berliners we met, yet by making the right decision we demonstrated to them that on the most fundamental level of human dignity we were. Through Frank's refusal we all understood that no wall could ever fully separate East from West. Fortunately, the view from the Wedels' fourth floor living room has changed. It now reveals a world where all of us can see the Rolling Stones, together, and listen to Mick Jagger as he sings, "You can't always get what you want, but if you try sometimes, you might find, that you get what you need."

SACHSENHAUSEN

CROSSING THE GATE:

In my three and half decades around the sun there have been exactly four times when I instinctively knew the events of the coming day would transform my life and change me on a most fundamental level. Three of them could be considered the clichés of life; the day Frank died, my first date with Julie (we have now been married 10 years), and the births of my two sons, Henry and Charlie (which I suppose is actually two days.) The remaining day was when my mom and I visited Sachsenhausen, the World War II concentration camp on the outskirts of Berlin.

I am not sure why the power of foresight was gifted to me on these occasions. Perhaps it was nothing more than an accident, an unexpected ray of morning sunshine illuminating my eyes at precisely the moment they opened. Or, was it the case that the events in my life had been building to a climatic apex, signaling a time of change, and that I understood that these days would bring a resolution that signaled the closing of one chapter in my life and the start of another? Or, maybe I didn't really possess this foresight at all, but invented it because the power of these four days were so critical to the story of me that I have simply chosen to remember them this way. Whatever the case may be, the day my mom and I visited Sachsenhausen is the first of the four.

I awoke almost paralyzed, afraid to face the coming day, yet paradoxically, eager to embrace it. I remained in bed for a few minutes trying to make sense of my heightened awareness and the unexpected anticipation that filled my thoughts. It was the middle of May and we only had a few weeks remaining before our odyssey was to end. I rose from bed and looked out the window to observe a colorful spring morning illuminated by the background of an immense blue sky. The gray blanket of the GDR winter had finally been lifted.

As we sat down to breakfast, my mom had a serious look on her face, and she began to tell me that today the two of us were going to visit Sachsenhausen, which was now a museum. She added that she had been thinking about this for a few weeks and finally decided that at nearly 11 years old, I was old enough to handle whatever we may see. It was important to her that I understand what actually happened in World War II as it was a part of both world history and my own. For my last name is Friedman, and my grandfather received a Purple Heart and Bronze Star in the War.

Before I knew it, the two of us were exiting the S-Bahn station and began the ten minute walk to Sachsenhausen. The walk filled me with wonder, for we were heading to a place of death; yet for those ten minutes our surroundings were so full of life. We were surrounded by the beauty of spring, the green emerging on the trees, birds chirping to one another and the picturesque cobblestone streets in front of vintage houses that lined the quiet family neighborhood. But when we made the last turn the magic of the moment suddenly disappeared.

At the end of the last row of houses stood a large gate. At the sight of it, an inner voice told me that if I stayed where I was, in the warm light of this beautiful day on the cobblestone street, I would be safe. But if I crossed the gate, I would enter into a new world, full of darkness and knowledge that I would wish I didn't possess.

We approached the gate and looked inside, pausing for a moment before crossing the line into the world it kept at bay. It was like we were in the Wizard of Oz, but in reverse. Behind us was the world of color, and in front of us the land of black and white. There was no vegetation, no life, nothing. Just brown dirt and fading grey structures that were preserved to keep the story of this place alive so that all who visited would never forget. Without stepping over the line, I observed East German soldiers walking around the grounds with their large German shepherds. I noticed the perimeter wall with barbed wire lining its top, and a large skull and crossbones painted on the section to my right. I looked back at the street behind us, wanting nothing more than to run to the nearest house, only meters away, for refuge. But I was here to learn about history, world history, my own history. I had a responsibility to continue. With great hesitation I took that fateful step forward.

THE OTHER SIDE:

As an adult I have visited the National Holocaust Museum in Washington D.C. twice. Both times I cried. But neither visit compares to my experience at Sachsenhausen. Looking back, I realize that at ten years old I was at an impressionable time in my life. It was a time where I was transitioning out of early childhood and just beginning to understand the immensity of the world and the concepts of history and time. Specifically, in traversing Sachsenhausen, I met its ghosts, which is an experience no museum can provide. To this day, if someone tells me they don't believe in ghosts, the rational part of me agrees, but there is another part of me that wants them experience Sachsenhausen as I did, for then they will believe:

THE BARRACKS:

We approached a building which we quickly understood to be the barracks for the Jews. It was heartbreaking. Their bunked beds were stacked so tightly it was as if they were coffins. At first it was difficult to fathom how so many people could fit into such a small room, but as if in answer to this question, there were large pictures exhibited adjacent to the bunks showing the starved prisoners who had once occupied this very room and stood on the very ground which was beneath me. I stared at the pictures of their half-dead faces and disintegrating malnourished bodies. Tears began to build, but I managed to keep them at bay. I then moved my eyes to view the entirety of the room itself. With the picture and the room now both within my field of vision, I could now see the barracks as they were, a half –century ago, in all its horror.

The combination of the visuals from the past and the physical remains of the present seemed to warp time itself. Together they forced me to understand the gravity of this place. I could feel its weight and the burden of its past on my shoulders. My eyes kept going back and forth between the defeated eyes of those in the pictures and the bunks in front of me, the same bunks that were in the picture, the same bunks in which the prisoners had slept. I found it unnerving how a picture from the past brought life, and in this case, death to the reality of the present. These bunks were not just part of the museum. I recognized them to be what they really were, the final resting place of those in picture.

As we turned to leave the bunks, we noticed a map of Europe on the wall. It was an interactive map which required that you push a button. I softly pushed the oversized red button and a few lights appeared on the map. They marked the locations of the large concentration camps, such as Auschwitz, in which hundreds of thousands were murdered. I pushed the button again. More lights came on. These were the mid-sized camps. I kept pushing the button until all the lights signifying the smaller camps were illuminated. When the last button was pushed, all of Europe was on display. Before our eyes was a map of an entire continent of death, with each light representing millions of pictures and bunks. (Note: according to the Sachsenhausen Museum Website, in 1992 an anti-Semitic fire bomb destroyed parts of Barrack 38 and 39).

The Ovens:

We found our way to the ovens. I distinctly recall a sense of physical fear coming over me as we walked around them and I learned of their significance. At ten years old, I had a limited understanding of life and death, but the meaning of the ovens was not lost on me. It felt as if the past horrors of Sachsenhausen were coming after me, for now I knew what happened here. It was paralyzing to stand in the same space where tens of thousands of individuals were murdered and then burned to ash while their captors laughed and celebrated the efficiency of their engineering.

At that moment, I asked myself how and why such brutality and violence could happen. It was beyond my comprehension how people could treat other human beings with such callousness and hatred that they would murder them then shove them into ovens, the same ovens that were now surrounding me. I pictured all the people, alone in the dark, yet with hundreds of others, waiting in fear to die. And the children, many my age or younger, crying and scared, holding their mothers hand, if they were lucky to have their mother with them. What did all the mothers say to all their children? What would my mom have said to me?

The Infirmary:

Of all my memories of Sachsenhausen, the infirmary is the most vivid. It was my experience here that haunted me long after I had left Berlin. In fact, even to this day, I am affected by what I saw and how, as I age and pass through time, my brief moments there altered my perception of life, death and humanity's struggle to understand both.

Everything was backwards. A hospital is supposed to be a place where the sick go to heal, where those in pain come to ease their suffering and where those who are dying do so with dignity. A hospital is a place where cleanliness and sterilization are necessities in order to protect the patients. But at Sachsenhausen, the infirmary and all its doctors established a house of horrors that brought death, pain and suffering. They worked in a clean and sterile environment not to protect the patients but to protect themselves from the uncleanliness of their patients.

As we walked around the ground floor operating room I noticed it was arranged as it would have been during the war. There was an operating table with medical instruments and lighting which looked much like a typical hospital setting today, just dated. However, the pictures and historical information displayed told the story of this place. The room we were standing in was used to conduct experiments on live individuals. I was drawn to the pictures and the suffering they depicted. I couldn't turn away. It was like the reflexive reaction we all get when encountering a fatal accident on the highway. It's impossible not to look at someone else's suffering. And in this moment, the associated guilt exploded within me due to my staring at the demise of another human being, even though it happened a half century earlier.

I wanted to burn the pictures - to erase them from my memory, to erase them from existence. To do so, I reasoned, would be to stop them from having ever occurred and thus would save the individuals trapped in them from their hideous fate. It would also save me from my fate of knowing what happened here. But this knowledge was the price of admission. And to destroy the pictures would be to permanently assign its victims to their fate, for they would be forgotten.

Although the photographs are permanently scarred into my memory, it is the knowledge that many of the experiments performed in the room were conducted by the infamous Dr. Mengele himself that haunts me. To know that I once walked where true evil both walked and thrived has been both a blessing and a curse. A blessing to have an understanding of what can happen in a world of indifference, yet a curse because that world, from so long ago, continues to find a way to surface.

As I continued to walk around the room, I noticed a set of stairs. With my mom still looking around the infirmary, I descended the steps by myself even though I was afraid of what I would find at the bottom. With each step my heart raced while my mind conjured up thousands of images of what awaited me in my descent, none of which were correct. I discovered a meticulous white tiled room with a slanted ceiling that extended to the ground at the far end. It was the room where they stored the bodies from above. The slant in the roof was the chute Mengele and others used to remove the dead from the chamber above. It was here that I observed the flowers.

It was a bouquet of brilliant red roses specifically placed where the slant of the roof met the cold tile floor. The roses brought the only color to this world of darkness in which I had descended. I wondered who had left them. I thought about the pain and suffering they still carried in their heart and the wounds that never healed in their soul. What pain would compel them, a half-century after the war, to come to this place? Was it a daughter, now grown and aged, remembering the father she never knew? Was it a wife telling her husband she still loved him through the passage of the decades? Was it a brother telling his sister he was sorry for not saving her and asking for her forgiveness? Was it an old man reaching across the boundaries of time to comfort his young imprisoned self with a reassurance that he would survive and endure?

A partial answer to my questions came about ten years later, when I watched *Schindler's List* for the first time. As the story unfolded, I was transported in time back to my childhood and that day in Sachsenhausen. When the girl's red coat was introduced I was stunned. Memories of the bouquet overwhelmed me. It was as if Spielberg had accessed one of the most powerful memories of my mind and displayed it for the world to see. For he got everything exactly right! The world of the concentration camps was filled with brutality, evil and indifference. It was a universe of black and grey, devoid of any color, except one, the color of the roses, the color of the coat, the color of blood. And this is where I found my answer. The coat and the roses belong to all of us, the living. They are both a part of our history and our future and we have a duty to never forget them.

My mom touched my shoulder. I didn't know how long she had been standing silently behind me, herself captured by the roses. Her touch signaled it was time to go home. I glanced over my shoulder as we walked up the steps, this time together, to see the roses one last time before they disappeared from view. We finally exited the infirmary and were back outside. I desperately wanted to go. Witnessing the barracks, the map, the ovens and the roses had changed me. We had to leave, at that very moment, or we would risk being trapped here ourselves. Sachsenhausen was not a museum and it lacked the safety that museums provide.

RETURN TO THE GATE:

We re-crossed the threshold of the gate and returned to Berlin and the cobblestone street neighborhood that was still filled with the colors of spring. But, the beautiful spring morning didn't seem as bright. The blue sky was not as brilliant. The emerging green on the trees and plants was not as joyous. As we turned the corner that finally took Sachsenhausen completely from our view, I felt a sense of relief. For, I had the sensation that it was watching me walk down the street and that it wasn't until I was out of its sight that I was truly free from its grasp. As my mom and I kept walking, neither of us with the power to say a word, the images of my two hours in Sachsenhausen formed a montage in my mind. I asked myself how people could be so cruel and inhumane to others. And that is when I finally understood the power and legacy of Sachsenhausen.

I realized that if this were 1938 rather than 1988 many people I know would never have been able to walk out those gates. I thought of my aunts and uncles back home. I pictured my cousin Stacie who was the same age as me, and my cousins Laura and Dane neither of whom was even five. They would have all been in the barracks or ovens or even worse, the infirmary. Then I thought of my dad, Herb. I couldn't understand how anyone, complete strangers no less, would want to hurt and kill him. Next I looked at my mom and realized that she too would never have left

Sachsenhausen, for she had married Jew. This revelation was devastating. I wanted to cry. But I didn't. I just kept walking because it was 1988 and not 1938. And in those final steps that morning I finally understood my family included me, for my last name is Friedman.

SECRET AGENT MAN

STAZI

There was no Constitution in East Berlin. No First or Fourth Amendments to protect the citizenry. Although we were Americans and enjoyed many privileges our status afforded us, we were still not immune to certain losses of liberty. We soon came to realize that while we were not at risk of disappearing to a labor camp we were more closely watched than the typical Berliner. We quickly learned that we could trust no one, for anyone could be Stazi. In fact, public records revealed after the end of communist rule that nearly 1 in 4 East Germans worked for the government in some type of informant capacity. Husbands and wives informed on each other, parents and children turned on one another, lifelong friends betrayed each other. This created a system, which Frank observed that "it didn't really matter if everyone was Stazi or no one was Stazi. Everyone had to be considered Stazi." This was true, especially for us.

(To get a more complete understanding of what life was like under constant surveillance, I recommend the excellent 2006 film "The Lives of Others" which perfectly captures what it was like to live in the constant state of fear and paranoia that was East Berlin.)

THE FOOTPRINT

It was early evening when we arrived back to our apartment in Marzahn. We had been away all day. Frank was teaching his class while my mom and I went exploring the University and city center. Upon our return we opened the door to our apartment and took a couple steps inside and immediately noticed something seemed off. At first we couldn't tell how, but we knew that someone had been in our apartment and looking through our personal possessions. Everything was in order, yet at the same time it wasn't. It was an eerie feeling, like we had been violated. We began to look around to make sure nothing was taken and to confirm that someone had actually been in our home.

Almost immediately we found the footprint. It was near the entrance to the living room. It was a large boot print formed in the layer of light dust that covered the ground. The three of us silently stared at the single print. This single boot print changed how we were to live for the next six months.

We would have preferred to have been robbed. But in our case, the intrusion was more disturbing. Nothing was missing. The stranger had entered for one purpose only, to get information, about us. We knew that somewhere there was a report filed on us and that another person or persons had access to our home anytime they wanted. Worse yet, this intruder was probably someone we knew.

With the discovery of the footprint we transitioned from the mentality of Americans to that of East Germans. We had to assume that everything we said and everything we did was being recorded. In response, we started searching the apartment for electronic surveillance devices or things that were out of place which could tell us what interested our unwelcome guest the most. It was rather comical, the three of us searching for electronic bugs, with only Hollywood spy movies to guide us in our search. We upended all the lamps, the beds the cabinets and couches. It was a fool's errand, since we had no idea what a small electronic recording device might look like, nor what we would do with one if we found it. To destroy it would only invite our anonymous guests back.

The single boot print forced us to adapt how we lived. What else could we do? From that moment on, anytime there was something important we needed to talk about, especially about life back home, we had code words. I was instructed to tell my mom that I thought we should go for a walk. If it was late, I would have to keep the thought inside my head until morning. Phone calls were now made only from the security of West Berlin. We trusted no one and, like Frank had said, everyone was Stazi.

Tomorrow Never Came

Down the street from our apartment in Marzahn, there was a neighbor-hood pub. With his Irish blood and outgoing personality, no matter where we traveled, Frank would always find a neighborhood pub and quickly assimilate with its patrons. Marzahn was no exception. It was through his lifelong journey to meet and learn the stories of others that Frank gave me one of the best pieces of advice I have ever received; if I really wanted to understand what is going on the world around me, I shouldn't listen to the academics with their heads up their asses. When I was old enough, I should go to a pub and have real conversation. He had learned more from pubs than he did from his decades in academia. In the case of East Berlin, the pub down the street was a treasure trove of knowledge.

A couple months into our stay, Frank was considered an honorary lo-cal by its staff and patrons. The bartenders and some of the regulars all knew him by name and welcomed him into their sanctuary. He became Norm from *Cheers*! For the East Berliners Frank was an interesting phe-nomenon. He was an American, said whatever the hell he wanted, but he was able to keep a balance and paradoxically be one of them. He never let his status as an American give off a perception that he was somehow better than anyone else in the pub. In a very real sense, the men of the pub taught Frank about everyday life for East Germans, and in return he taught them the same about Americans. The East-West divide was breaking down one Pilsner and one conversation at a time. As the friendships formed, it was easy to forget that everyone was Stazi.

Frank bonded particularly well with one of the bartenders, Michael. He was a young man, single, in his late twenties and could be considered an East German hipster. One night the drinks were flowing and the conversation among Frank, Michael and the other regulars became particularly lively and animated. Eventually, they turned to Rock and Roll which seemed to happen frequently in East Berlin. Rock and Roll was one of the few Western concepts that the East Germans could talk about in public as long as they stuck to the music and not the messages.

As the good times rolled the lively discussion about the Stones, Springsteen, the Clash and others filled the confines of the pub. With each Pilsner, Stazi receded in the minds of Michael, Frank and the others. Eventually, as Frank was preparing to leave, he was invited by Michael to get together the next day to listen to some music and carry on the conversation. The invitation was accepted.

Frank never saw Michael again. After that night there was no more jolly laughter with his comrades in the pub. Frank was no longer Norm. Now he was greeted with a simple hello when he walked in and maybe some talk about the weather. He would order a Pilsner, give a nod to his comrades, then quietly give a second nod to Michael, where ever he was.

SAY CHEESE

It was May 1st 1988, May Day. The day the rest of the world celebrates the labor of the working class. This was an especially important holiday in the Communist bloc. There was a parade and rally taking place near Alexanderplatz and we decided that we should go and experience it. We met up with a few of our American friends we had met who were living in East Berlin and we all traveled to Alexanderplatz together.

The streets were jammed with people and noise. It seemed as if the whole city had come down to its center to celebrate labor. But the parade and marches were not simply to acknowledge the work of the people, they were to pay respect to the Communist Party. To not attend would be noticed, for everyone was Stazi.

There was a group of about 8 of us Americans. We were walking among the scores of people, taking pictures and following the lead of the crowds. We knew we were being watched, but that was nothing new. However, in this case, we actually identified the Stazi who was following us! We decided to have some fun with him.

He was a middle age man, with graying hair, slender with the tough dehydrated skin of a smoker. He had been following us for some time when we finally noticed that every time we stopped, he would stop. After a few blocks of our game of cat and mouse our group gathered at a corner and turned our backs to him. With our backs shielding us we grabbed our cameras then pretended like we were going to start walking again. After a few steps we suddenly turned. Say Cheese! We all waved at him and our cameras began clicking away.

The Stazi-man quickly disappeared into the crowd but not before our cameras permanently caught his snarling response. With our friend now gone, we continued on our way, with our cameras ready as we tried to determine who else among the crowd was assigned to watch us.

AMERIKA

As I look back on my life, I am always bewildered by what events I actually remember. Why is it that some events which seem to be life-changing at the time are quickly forgotten while others which, in the grand scheme of life, are seemingly so unimportant yet vividly recalled decades later? How is it that I can't remember something that happened just a few days ago, but I distinctly recall events from years ago? For example, I can't tell you for the life of me what I had for dinner last Tuesday, yet I know that in 1988 Will Smith told me that "Parents Just Don't Understand", George Michael told me to have "Faith" and Tom Selleck, Ted Danson and Steve Guttenburg had a baby. I also know that the 5th grade students of Steve Berghdahl's class played two-hand touch football at lunch every day with one kid missing.

In trying to answer the questions of how and why I remember and forget, I have come across a theory which postulates that "out of ordinary" experiences rewire your brain. During these times, memories are stored differently which affects how they are later recalled (or forgotten). A common example is a traumatic experience that haunts a survivor years later. However, in the case of our travels to East Berlin, a more applicable analogy is that of vacation. Vacations are times when we leave our daily routine for new and exciting experiences. I recall with great detail many vacations I went on as both a child and adult, whether it was a simple camping trip or traveling overseas, yet I very rarely recall the weeks and months surrounding those trips. The case of Berlin was no different. In my mind it has become an extended vacation. But as with any vacation, it is always nice to return home.

In Berlin, home was never far from our thoughts. Whether it was keeping up with our family, friends or pop-culture, we tried to stay abreast of life back in the U.S. As the three of us quickly discovered, our time living outside the U.S. afforded a unique opportunity to understand our home and our own lives from a new perspective – that of an outsider. While this might not seem like something of great significance, it is perhaps the single most important occurrence in my own story. For in seeing the United States from an outsider's perspective I was really observing myself from the reference point of another person and another culture. This extraordinary opportunity to see myself outside myself at such a young age was truly a transformative experience that has impacted me to this day. At that specific time however, as the days turned to weeks and months, and we observed from afar the routine of daily life back home, this revelation had not yet taken hold of me. I wanted nothing more than to leave Berlin. The mundane of life back home became exciting. Perhaps it was this excitement upon hearing news from California that rewired my memory. While I may never understand how or why I recall specific memories, I possess a random collection nonetheless, from which I try to make sense. The following are some of the most vivid memories of life back in California and the U.S. from my vantage point of East Berlin. They are collectively titled "Amerika".

American Forces Network

"This is Carmen Walker taking you home; from the edge."

I eagerly anticipated those words every night. They were broadcast from the American Military Base in West Berlin. Their nightly arrival signaled the momentary escape from my confines of East Berlin and the apartment in Marzahn and bought me on a brief trip back to California. It was the hour before bed time when my mom, Frank and I would listen as AFN radio filled our apartment with the songs that were topping the charts back home. For sixty precious minutes (or 3,600 seconds, but who was counting) our tiny dreary silent apartment in Marzahn would transform into an island of American pop culture. For that one hour we were joined in Marzahn by the likes of George Michael, INXS, George Harrison, Rick Astley, Will Smith, Aerosmith, The Beach Boys, Whitney Houston, Guns and Roses others. It was as if all of them were performing their songs just for us.

The three of us would sit on our sofa listening to the music, taking notes of new songs on the charts and those that were fading into the dustbin of Billboard trivia history. The time we spent together with our musician friends was about much more than just music, it was about connecting with our friends and family back home. I always imagined my buddies hanging out after school, listening to the local radio station and singing along to their favorite songs, while they traded baseball cards and talked about who was hotter, Samantha Fox or Belinda Carlisle. This was the stuff that really mattered in our lives. Just because I was alone in a far off place didn't mean these things stopped mattering. I always wondered if the songs that became my favorites were the same as theirs and if they would make fun of me because I preferred Belinda.

It was over the course of these one hour vacations where I slowly awakened to the transformative power of music. The songs I heard took me to places I never imagined and let me escape from East Berlin. The lyrics captured thoughts that were bottled up inside me which I was afraid to share, such as the fact that, at least for the first month, I wanted nothing more than to go home; and I hated my mom and Frank for taking me to this God awful place. But where I could not speak for myself, the music spoke for me.

I specifically remember the first time I heard Will Smith calmly and collectedly tell me that "parents just don't understand." I was floored! How could he say that and get away with it? It was completely true and the most profound statement my 10 year old ears had ever heard! It was something I felt deep inside me, it was something I wanted to scream but never could, for if I did my parents would make me eat soap like Ralphie in *A Christmas Story*. But now I didn't need to say it. Will said it for me. All I had to do was silently smile at my mom and Frank and let Will take the punishment.

But it wasn't just Will, it was all them. I marveled at how all these songs and the people who sang them could speak to and for me. How they could connect me to my friends even though we were separated by two continents and divided by the Cold War. The music transcended everything because for that one hour it became everything. Somehow, the songs that Carmen sent us bridged this divide and in doing so, she really did send us home.

DALLAS

One of the advantages of living in East Berlin as opposed to anywhere else in East Germany or the Soviet Bloc, was that West Berlin controlled the airwaves. Try as they might, the East Germans could not stop the television and radio broadcasts streaming from West Berlin. It was a non-stop bombardment of Western culture that included not only AFN radio, but many American television shows. In 1988, while the U.S. watched the final season of *Magnum P.I.* and felt at home with the regulars of *Cheers*, East Berliners were watching too. But it was the night time soaps such as *Knotts Landing, Dallas* and *Dynasty* that captured the imagination of our East German friends and their perception of daily life in America.

The East Berliners viewed America as the land of J.R. Ewing's and the mega mansions of *Dallas*. The lifestyles they saw depicted on night-time soaps were a fantasy world they turned into the reality in which all Americans lived. Most had never met an American, so their perceptions were warped by what they saw on their black and white screens. This led our East German friends to initially be incapable of understanding that the life depicted in Dallas was as foreign to us as it was to them. They questioned us on how we could live in America, the land of opportunity, and not live like the Ewings. All Americans were like the Ewings they insisted. You must have great houses and cars and walk around with your own theme songs playing in the background they joked. For you are Americans.

Perhaps purposefully, they chose not to believe us when we told them that most Americans were middle class and worked long hours to afford modest homes, save for their kids college education and a yearly vacation. They did not understand when we told them that, yes there was great wealth like they saw on *Dallas*, but there was also great poverty. It was the discussions about poverty that perplexed them the most, for in East Berlin there was no great wealth, but there was also an absence of poverty. They could not fathom how America could be the land of freedom and opportunity, yet have so many of its citizens living in conditions worse than those in the GDR. What they didn't understand was that America was a place of great contradiction for freedom necessitates this paradox.

Only through the course of time and the ensuing trust that came through the strengthening of friendships with the East Berliners did their understanding of actual life in the U.S. begin to change. They reluctantly accepted that our freedom provided us with grand opportunity, but nothing was guaranteed. With this revelation, they realized that most Americans were not like the Ewings, they were like my mom, Frank and me. And with all of us getting to know each other intimately over the months, it was apparent that we, the everyday people of the East and West, actually had more in common than not.

MAGIC (JOHNSON)

Growing up in Southern California during the 1980's there was no one more exciting than Magic Johnson and the Showtime Lakers. Magic, with his larger than life persona and infectious smile led what every kid knew was the greatest basketball team ever. Our love for Magic and the Lakers was rivaled only in our hatred for Larry Bird and the Boston Celtics. However, it was a hatred born from respect. Both this respect and hatred came from a history long before us kids were born. It was a history that captured our imagination in the 1980's as we witnessed each Lakers Celtics battle. Their legacy became ours. However, in 1988, the year we were in Berlin, the NBA of the 80's came to close and sadly, the Lakers and Celtics would not meet again for two decades.

It was that year when a part of my childhood, along with most kids in Southern California, ended. The villains were the Bad Boy Detroit Pistons with their rough style of play that brought in a new era in the NBA, and looking back, a new era in American pop culture that would come to personify the early 1990's and my teenage years. It was this year that the Pistons finally beat the Celtics and the following year in 1989 they would topple the Lakers. But 1988 belonged to Magic, Kareem and giants of the Showtime one last time. And I had a front row seat that was just 6,000 miles away to witness firsthand the Bad Boys lose in seven games, while the Lakers became the first team to win back to back championships in twenty years, a standard by which all championship teams are now measured.

It was around 10:00 each night when the games would stream over AFN radio into our tiny Marzahn apartment. My mom and Frank would go off to bed and I would be alone, in the living room anticipating the tip off. Frank with his Irish ancestry and allegiance to the Celtics could not bear to listen to the games with me; for it was the same Magic who defined my childhood that also ended his extended adolescent years. In Frank's world there were only two teams that mattered in the NBA, the Celtics and the Lakers and the Lakers always lost to the Celtics. This ended with Magic's Jr. Skyhook in 1984. So I listened to the 1988 games alone, yet alongside everyone I knew back home.

Games 6 and 7 were in Los Angeles with the Bad Boys up three games to two. If the Lakers lost either game it was over. When game 6 came finally across the air waves, a rush of excitement filled the air. I could hear the crowd in the background and feel the energy of the Great Western Forum and all of Southern California crossing two continents as it filled Marzahn. It was the middle of the night in Berlin, but I was home in sunny Southern California.

The games always magically transported me. Despite being nearly 6,000 miles away, we were all together, in unison cheering Magic, Kareem, Worthy and the rest of the Showtime crew. My dad had written me that he was going to tape the games for me so we could watch them when I got home. These games were everything to me, especially game 6. Game 6 wasn't just about the Lakers beating the Pistons, it was about giving me one more night back home. It was also about having the chance to stick it to Mr. Solomon.

Mr. Solomon and his wife were Americans who lived directly underneath us in Marzahn. They also happened to be from Detroit and were huge Pistons fans. The Solomons were some of the only Americans we met in East Berlin for obvious reasons that escaped me at the time. I just knew them as the nice old Jewish couple from Detroit. Although we got along great, when it came to our teams battling for the NBA championship, niceness went out the window.

After each of the first 5 games, Mr. Solomon and I would stare each other down the next day. I was Dennis the Menace to his Mr. Wilson. With each Pistons win, he would give me his old man stare trying to put me in my place, telling me that my beloved Lakers and Southern California were finally heading for a spectacular fall. It was a stare that told me I was just a bratty spoiled kid who knew nothing about winning and losing and the long suffering years of a team with no championships. With each Lakers win, I would give him my ten year old smirk and remind him that his team hadn't won a championship once during his first six decades on this planet and they weren't going to do it this year. Not in LA or Berlin.

When the Pistons went up 3-2 it was tough to deal with him. He began talking to me in the days between, trying to make me doubt the Lakers. He was especially harsh toward Magic, to whom he kept referring as "Tragic Johnson". As a Lakers fan, and especially a Magic fan, those were fighting words, for nobody messed with Magic. I had to defend Magic from Mr. Solomon. I couldn't let some old man from Detroit bad mouth my hero. I knew my dad and my friends were counting on me. But, all I could muster in response was, "You haven't won yet. Have you forgotten game 6 and 7 are in LA?" It wasn't the best come back, but it was the truth and it stung him just a little because he had thought I would cower, that I would have doubts but I didn't. I was too young to doubt and didn't know any better. The naivety of youth was my ace in the hole in this game of wits with Mr. Solomon and it drove him crazy.

I was hoping for a blowout victory in game 6. My nerves couldn't take a close game. Instead it was one of the most memorable and exciting games in NBA history. The entire game was back and forth. My knees were shaking and body was sweating from the hours of jumping around while I silently screamed. In the third quarter Isaiah Thomas had what is still an NBA record 25 points, most of it on a severely sprained ankle. With his performance, it seemed as if the gods were not with the Lakers and they had decided to make Isaiah and the Pistons not just champions, but legends. For the very first time, the thought that the Lakers might lose had entered my mind as a distinct possibility, along with having to deal with a gloating Mr. Solomon.

The break between the third and fourth quarters was agonizing. Since I was listening to the radio rather than watching television, my imagination had been running wild in a way that television inhibits. I had to imagine each shot, each dribble, each pass. I had to imagine the crowd and Jack Nicholson. I had to imagine Pat Riley giving the orders in the huddle on how to attack the final 12 minutes. It seemed like hours before the announcers began the play by play of the 4th quarter.

Once the game resumed it continued to be a match of titans. Then the final minute arrived and the Lakers were down by three. It was nervous time. Byron Scott hit a jumper to cut it to one and before I knew it, there was a flurry of action and the announcers were suddenly screaming the Lakers won by a single point! Detroit had failed to score on the last possession of the game. I started running around the apartment, jumping on the couch, joining in the frenzy I heard on the radio. We now had game seven and there was no doubt who was going to win. I knew it, Mr. Solomon knew it, my friends knew it and my dad did too. And there I was, after midnight, connecting on invisible high fives that reached from Berlin to LA. It truly was a Magic moment.

LETTERS FROM HOME

March 31, 1988

Dear Celeste and Eric,

The class has really enjoyed hearing from you. We appreciate you taking the time to write and to keep us up to date on what you've been doing.

It truly must be an "experience" to live in East Germany. Your letters have been followed by good class discussion based on what you've told us about your visit. I'm glad to hear, Eric, that you're able to get to and from school on your own and that you're taking your German seriously.

I wonder what it will be like coming back to American schools in the fall? Surely many of the things you're learning now will help you to be an even better student next year.

Your letters describe pretty much what I expected your visit would be like. I am surprised however at some of the inconveniences brought about by shortages of food and raw materials. Funny how we Americans take so much for granted.

I get the impression that Eric and his books are a little like Abe Lincoln of 130 years ago – enjoying what one has access to. I'm glad you enjoyed "21 Balloons" and "Ishi" so much.

In school we're a couple days away from our Easter break. I hope the accompanying letters, Eric, will give you an idea how the kids have been doing. We seem to have several aspiring "Rona Barrett" types, so who likes who will be obvious and you'll not feel left out. Does the "Boy/Girl Spring Time Flu" also attack German children? If so, let us know. Some things are universal.

Our trip to Catalina was really outstanding! We took 116 kids and 5 teachers accompanied by about 10 parents. The weather was perfect and the activities just right. Every day we spent snorkeling in the water with 20 to 30 visibility or hiking around a lush green island. I hope as a 6th grader, Eric, you'll get a chance to do this next year. It surely is a highlight for a grammar school career. Everybody's knowledge of the ocean was greatly enhanced by the trip.

Of course, we are all saddened by the fact the Dr. Ehrenborg is retiring. The principal selection process is now going on. The ability of any one person to take Dr. E's place would seem impossible. Everyone is apprehensive about what changes might take place in school. I think the best thing we can do is keep an open mind and give the new principal a chance to succeed. I believe flexibility still remains one of the important elements to a successful life.

In closing, I want to again thank you for your communication with the class and what's going on with you in East Germany. It sounds as if you are taking every opportunity to get the most from your visit, and I look forward to seeing you in the fall and hearing more stories about your wonderful experience.

Happy Easter and have an enjoyable spring time!

Sincerely,

Steve Bergdahl

March 31, 1988

Dear Eric,

Hi Eric, this your best friend Daniel. What's it like up there? School is great. You want to know something? Tim got a girlfriend. At school we don't play football that much anymore. It's different without you. How many kids are in your class? Don't forget that if you do find a girlfriend you owe me two dollars. Well, Eric, I miss you. We always had the best of times. Don't you wish that we could still get in trouble? I do.

    Later Dude,
    Daniel

March 31, 2014

Dear Mr. Bergdahl,

I apologize that it has taken me so long to respond to your letter from March 31, 1988. It is difficult to believe that a quarter century has passed since you wrote to me and included letters from my fifth grade class. When I woke this morning and reread your letter, which had miraculously survived twenty five years of multiple moves, I decided that it was finally time send you a reply.

I will start by sincerely thanking you for taking the time to write me so many years ago. Your letter and those of my classmates means as much to me now as it did then. I remember the excitement of that day in 1988 when we received the package of letters from home. It was early April and while I had become accustomed to life in East Berlin there was naturally a part of me that wished I was still at home, in your class, with all my friends, playing football with the guys and keeping up with the latest gossip, or even being the latest gossip. At the time, I did read your letter, but the truth is, most of it glossed over me. I thought it was cool that you, my teacher, wrote me, but I was much more interested in what my friends had to say. After all, the news from my friends was much more interesting than the articulate words of my teacher! But today, as I reread your letter, I finally came to appreciate your words as much as theirs.

You see, I also remember the day, not too long ago, when I found the package of letters sitting in box in my closet. I was cleaning out old papers and came across the manila envelope with air mail stamps and my Berlin address. (Can you believe it only cost $2.50 to express mail a package with 25 pages from California to East Berlin!) When I saw the wrinkled envelope a rush of emotions and excitement overcame me as I realized what its precious contents were. I am sure you can imagine how miraculous it was to unexpectedly find such a magical package that included your letter and the accompanying letters from all my friends at the time, friends who are now in their mid-thirties like I am. As I opened the letters, childhood memories, of both Santa Barbara and Berlin, overwhelmed me. My past revealed itself to me in a manner I had never thought possible. And for this, I am ever grateful to you. Your foresight to send me the letters enabled me to receive them twice, both then and now.

As I made my way through the letters and specifically reread your letter from the perspective of a mid-thirties adult who is a husband and father of two boys, I realized the true power of letters in and of themselves. Letters, such as yours, paradoxically both transcend and capture time. The thoughts, emotions and daily details of life that are forever inked on the page are read and re-read throughout the years, each time transforming its recipient and bringing a new level of understanding. In fact, I believe that letters are more powerful than photographs, for they capture the inner spirit of the individual who writes them at a specific time in their life while also allowing them to communicate to its recipient decades later. How is it possible that the words you wrote to me in 1988 have come to form an entirely different letter in 2014? As a confused boy, I missed most of what you had to say, but as a man I understand what you wrote and what you were telling me. And that is the magic of your letter; it has enabled you and me to communicate as two adults, roughly the same age, separated only by time. Isn't it truly a shame that nobody writes letters anymore?

So this is why I write you today, to hopefully repay you by offering you the excitement of an unexpected letter arriving in your mail box. I wish I could be there to see you as you tear the seal of the envelope and begin to read these words and recall events from a quarter century ago. I think that both of us would agree it is difficult to comprehend how the passage of time enables me to today hold the very letters that you and a room full of children once held, letters that I held as a child myself, in a place that now only exists in the context of history books and memory. How is it that these simple letters have outlasted the mighty Berlin Wall and Soviet Communism?

In closing, I sincerely thank you for your letter and those of my childhood friends, which I have enclosed for you to read, for they are as much yours as mine. Please know, they gave me great comfort both then and now, and through them I have come to understand how much the world and I have changed since the day in which they were written.

Your fifth grade student,

Eric Friedman

AUFWIEDERSEHEN

Aufwiedersehen is one of the more poetic words of the harsh sounding German language. When broken down it is actually three separate words: Auf (until), wieder (again), sehen (to see). In English this roughly translates to "until we see each other again", however this literal meaning strips it of its essence.

Aufwiedersehen is a beautiful word, that for me captures the whole of the human experience, for nothing is truly permanent, even a city with a wall. We live in a constantly changing world where each moment we say goodbye to our surroundings. It's as if everything around is constantly dying, being moved to the dustbins of our collective memory while at the same time being reborn into the life of our current collective experience. With today's modern technology all but eliminating permanence yet permanently recording each moment of our lives, can we ever truly say goodbye?

My experiences from those six months in the Berlin of 1988 tell me no, for to say goodbye is to acknowledge an end point in time. Yes, people may leave us, objects may come and go, cities may disappear, yet they don't just cease to be. When the Wall came down on November 9, 1989, the city that defined the physical and political wars of the twentieth century came to an end, it took its last breath, for it truly was a living entity, not an inanimate object. And on that day a quarter century ago, Berlin left the world of the living and became a myth, a myth that lives on in memory.

While the Berlin I came to know and love as a child is no longer, it continues to visit me in both my thoughts and dreams. I experience it through recollections of friendship. I hear it in the stories of my mother. I see it when visiting Frank at the cemetery. I recognize its imprint in the man I have become. After twenty five years all I can really say is thank you Berlin and Aufwiedersehen.

CELESTE

GHOST STATIONS AND
DESERT DOGS

Journal Entry: Sunday, January 31, 1988

I listened to Alistair Cook's "America" on the BBC. I've never listened to a radio show before. The difference between the radio and television I've discovered: language. I heard the ways he used words, and I could follow the transitions in thought. It wasn't simply that he was English. There was no suit of clothes, or background set, or even a smile to distract me. Only his voice.

I'm like a child in a grown person's body. It's all a wonder to me, but I'm old enough to feel the wonder and question it and understand it. I have much to write down already and want to, while I still live in No Man's Land. Perhaps, my entire visit here I will live in that place. I must work on my burrow.

Step back in time to 1988 Berlin – to the Berlin that is relegated to history – and imagine yourself on the U- Bahn, Berlin's underground rail system. The train is packed with Germans fortunate to possess transit passports. Most are old women from the East who purchase candy and cheap goods in the western sectors. Old people because they would not be missed if they stayed in the West, their pensions forfeit. (Curiously, the women never bring back fresh fruits and vegetables. Fruit from Israel is *verboten*; the Palestinian *Intifada* in the news daily.) One overhears snippets of conversation among the passengers. Then, SILENCE. Only the

111

clackety-clack of the train along the tracks, a sound amplified in the emptiness outside.

Our train is passing underneath No Man's Land. You recognize it by the ghost stations: abandoned subway platforms except for the solitary guard posted in what once was the ticket booth. All around a stillness, such that even the dust had settled long before. But first, you recognize the station by the split-second silence that always precedes entry to this solitary place. It's a silence that envelopes the subway car. The train whisks past, and there is this quiet, both within and without, for just those moments of transit between two worlds, East / West. Clackety-clack. It's as if you are descending into a tomb. No one moves. No one speaks, not even the children. We turn toward the window and look beyond without appearing to look. I recall lines from a Frost poem: "They cannot look out far. / They cannot look in deep. . . ." I peer through the sooty glass, past my own ghostly reflection and then to the young border guard holding his semi-automatic.

I never experienced greater dread than during those moments of intersection with the ghost stations. My father was to experience same when he, Cold Warrior, visited us at the end of our stay in June 1988. My Dad had fought in the 102nd Infantry, Rhineland Campaign. His entire career was in Defense technology, developing laser optics for satellite cameras and weaponry. That was his camera on the front page photo of the New York *Times*, the famous Khrushchev shoe-banging incident. But when we transported him from Tegel Airport to the outskirts of Berlin in Marzahn, I catalogued a fear in his eyes that I had seen from him never.

And yet, I miss that Berlin, Berlin in 1988 and just 18 months before *Die Wende* – The Turning.

One year previous, the decision to apply for the Fulbright teaching exchange had been mine. And like the few really monumental decisions in my life, it was impulsive. I was the gut instinct member of our marital duet. *Just run with it!* And that is how I reacted the day when Frank brought home the letter of invitation handed him by his department chair, Porter. For both colleagues, the letter was given and accepted as a good joke. In reading the letter of invitation, I had no illusions that my husband had been the first and only choice his chair bothered to consider. A sabbatical to the Eastern Bloc? English Department colleagues would finagle sabbatical leaves in France, Italy, the UK, and Greece, too, depending on the politics. East Germany? Even West Germany wasn't much of a draw in 1987. And so, the invitation was passed along as though an aside – "Oh by the way, Frank.... " Upon our return, it was the same from the UCSB colleagues, no one much interested. Just a shrug, we might as well have returned from a sabbatical in San Berdu. Even the German Studies Department on campus declined our gift of GDR books, books brought back for them, including several by the celebrated novelist, Christa Wolf.

But in reading the USIA letter, my mongrel spirit had been triggered. I imagined us there already. To be invited to live in a communist country! Actually *invited* behind the Wall: *Die Maurer.* "Go for it, Frank!" I didn't even consider the complications of a move that was literally from one world to another. I was in the moment, let's run! You. Me. Eric. Run!

I recalled that impulse this past spring. I had taken in the new photography exhibit at the Santa Barbara Art Museum: John Divola's Southern California photographs of abandoned houses around and about Los Angeles. In the last gallery, I was particularly drawn to pictures of Mojave desert dogs, photos taken of dogs in hot pursuit of the photographer, as he sped his car with camera side-mounted, past desolate housing encampments on the outskirts of the southern California desert. One photo in particular captures the essence in a bigger than life shepherd-mix – *the in-the-moment doggie-ness* – as he races alongside the speeding car, futile though it be. All four legs off the ground, tail straight out behind, and its eyes penetrating the camera lens. No thought to why or where-for. Divola's car speeds alongside, parallel to the racing dog.

In that museum gallery, I came to see myself reflected, my mongrel self, racing in the moment again, back to when Frank handed me the Fulbright letter.

I did compromise in one area, though. We decided against a full year and opted instead for a one-semester commit in East Germany's capital. Spring semester 1988, one of the pivotal years in GDR history. First, there was *Glasnost*—the Soviet policy of openness under the Gorbachev regime. This would have applied to virtually the entire Eastern bloc, save Rumania and Albania, and would have accounted for the exchange through the USIA. Our family of three became a tiny piece of Gorbachev's openness policy. Secondly, the Palestinian *Intifada*, predictably pitting East (pro-Palestinian) against West (pro-Israeli). So we arrived in the GDR at a time of simultaneously coming together, but also pulling apart.

And we had chosen the city in the center of it all: Berlin. Throughout our months there, we could feel the pulling together/coming apart as we were caught in that tension. Fulbrighters, we were neither State Department nor Socialist. We were between two worlds, but not exactly *in* them. Our lives were as surreal as the new world we now inhabited.

Berlin in 1988 was truly the center of the world, the Cold War world. There were the missiles to prove it. Short-range missiles pointed at the city from the Soviet-controlled East and facing our own missiles from the West. Then the medium-range missiles further out, Western Europe and Eastern Bloc. Ultimately, the big boys at home deep in Russian territory and scattered across the continental U.S., including those missiles stored beneath the ground at Vandenberg AFB, just north of our Santa Barbara home. At least in my imagination. And all of them, pointed, at the three of us. At least in one's imagination.

A TOUCH OF GRAY

DDR paradox came back at me later that evening in our neighborhood Bier Stube. We shared our table with two German couples, and I could see that the men were already snockered. Naturally, our English interested them and we struck up conversation. It was the usual chit chat and cross-language struggle until Frank realized what the one fellow – the drunker of the two, therefore, the more embittered one, had been saying. That we were able to visit Berlin from California; but that he could not visit California from the DDR. I had Frank translate for me, "But that is the reason we are here in Berlin. So that someday YOU can travel to the U.S."

I'm afraid it didn't help much. And it struck me that the majority of these people do live in a prison. If you put up bars, you have made a prison. It makes no difference what the world behind those bars is. All that matters is the impenetrability of the wall.

We haven't seen the bars because they don't exist for us. We return home in five months. That must be why we haven't bothered to visit the wall yet. Our first trip to West-Berlin, it never occurred to me to walk to the wall and touch it, estimate its height, speculate on its composition. Understand the cost in human blood.

Every picture I'd ever had in my head about East Berlin has been colored in gray. The varying shades that I recall from post-war movies like Carol Reed's *The Third Man*. Or scenes from Cold War thrillers of the 1960's, double-agents walking across Checkpoint Charlie in the dark of night, usually after a hard rain for visual effect and sound effects, the splashing of hurried footsteps across cobblestoned streets. So as we were driven that wintry morning, across the border and into the East, I could see that my image of Berlin was absolutely bang on. It was as though we were now transported into a grainy black and white movie. The speckled snow, then sludge; the concrete *Neues Bauen* high rises, the landscape dotted with barren trees, still sparse even after forty years. As the weeks passed and winter gave way to spring, the greyness would stubbornly persist. Blustery March winds from the Soviet plains to the east whirled the coal dust into clouds all about the city. I was not to lose my coal-dust cough for a full two years, the gray carried within me for months after our departure.

I like to think that our American-ness brought color to Berlin *Hauptstadt*. The Yankee spirit of not taking ourselves or the world too seriously, something Germans – East or West – could never comprehend. I thought it funny, still do, that the West German chancellor's name, "Kohl," translated to "cabbage" in English: "Helmut Cabbage." *Blumen kohl; Rosen kohl; Weiss kohl*: The German equivalent of a salad bar. I'd share the joke with the Berliners, but they never got the humor of it, instead returning a befuddled look absent of any reaction. Hunh? Ironic that the American they'd invited to teach at Humboldt was himself the quintessential jokester.

Then there was another time, when our brashness cost and did cost someone dearly. The *Bier Tulpe*, a German pub, was situated on the ground floor of our apartment building. (In a land of shortages, the *Bier Stube*, or neighborhood bar, was plentiful.) We'd regularly show up there, sometimes as a family for a midday meal. Other times, just Frank and myself to enjoy a mug of Berliner Pilsener. Soon after our arrival, we latched onto one of the three men working there, Mike, for Mikhail, who tended bar with "Baldy" and "Toothless." Mike was the youngest of the three waiters, still single and in awe of us, his first direct link to American culture. He was fascinated particularly by Frank. Together, they would chat or more often than not, argue about western rock music, especially on the days when Frank would carry along a cassette or two to share with him. Then Mike would cock his head, trying to keep up with the frumpled man before him, Frank always relaxed, holding court, just as he had with his students at Woodstock's Pizzeria in Isla Vista.

So we really didn't give it much of a thought when Mike invited us to visit him at his flat the following evening. I still have it marked on my calendar: "Mike – 8:00," Tuesday, March 22nd. We'd bring along a selection of cassettes and contribute bottles of Pilsener. The waiter's building was just a short 5-minute walk from our own. I sensed, though, before we even knocked on the door, that he wouldn't answer. I had felt the uneasiness hours earlier at home still, while Frank selected from among our cassettes: Dire Straits, Phil Collins, Stevie Winwood, *Clapton*. Top of the stack, absolutely frozen in memory: Steely Dan's *Gaucho*. The hallway outside Mike's flat was empty, the silence unsettling me. Just the sound of Frank knocking, softly. Pause. Several more tentative knocks. But quiet all around. Was our waiter behind the door? Or was it empty space beyond us? We stood quietly for just about another minute although it seemed interminable at the time. I couldn't even look at Frank, nor him at me. By this time in the stay, even Eric knew the times when silence was in order. Another wall between them and us.

The next day, Mike was gone, and we didn't ask why at the B*ier Stube*. We learned later that one of the other two waiters was *Stasi*, the one Frank had nicknamed "Toothless."

The two sides to the Wall – *Die Maurer* – likewise reflected the colorless / colorful distinguishing East and West. The Berlin Wall was actually a number of walls. The East whitewashed without so much as a scratch mark on it, anywhere, ever. Just crumbling concrete and the pervasive coal soot. Then a bit beyond, another wall parallel to the first. Beyond, No Man's Land: empty save for the birds that fly over the treeless stretch and the lone armed border soldier. And unseen, mines below the grasses; further along, the guard towers positioned at regular intervals for miles.

At the farthest side of No Man's Land, the *famous* wall. Every available space graffito, the entire stretch of the wall as it continued for miles. In its way, the colorful patchwork of obscenities and political slogans represented a sort of palimpsest, the imposition of West over the East. Paint on Drab. Excess super-imposed on Sparing. We saw it in West Berlin's buildings, too, modern built next to restored, next to ruins. Color everywhere: on the billboards, the tiled roofs, the brightly attired inhabitants and visitors. Colors and colorful among the great variety of life in the west. Fabulous, exotic foods. Ka-De-Ve Department Store – stories high and even more decadent than Chicago's downtown Marshall Fields -- its top floors devoted to food stuffs from everywhere! One entire section dedicated to the salami, hundreds of varieties. (Our favorite, the sweet

Hungarian.) Turks selling spicy gyros just blocks from the border, sliced to order from beef slabs rotisserie cooked all the day long, the smell of it wafting across the street – yes, actually "wafting." And those treks to the little camera store visible to me as I crossed over through Checkpoint Charlie. I'd shop in the West to purchase Japanese brand color film, only black and white available in the East. There it was again, that color distinction between East and West. How provincial East Berlin appeared to me, compared to the West! Even on a late Saturday night where the West was just coming alive, our streets were already quiet, few cars in sight. An entire city already tucked in for the night, silence except for the drunken chatter escaping from the doorways of the scattered *Bier Stubes* and the few privately-owned restaurants downtown. It was as though time had stopped forty years earlier in this one sector of the world. We found ourselves caught between those two worlds: East and West. The one, a Technicolor spectacle. Ours, a photograph from an old family album.

We could feel that same disconnectedness in our relations with both Humboldt University and the U.S. Consulate. Indeed, we found ourselves relegated to that in-betweenness throughout our six-month stay. Because we weren't American CP (Communist Party), Frank's German colleagues and students wouldn't – or couldn't – fraternize with us, except as a collective and in official settings. When I invited them to Frank's birthday party in late May, the American Studies chair, Christopher Mueller, issued a directive. Two dozen faculty and students showed up together; then two hours later, just as abruptly left. There was their suspicion, not without precedent, I suspect, that as we were under the USIA, we were possibly more State Department than Academia. Surprisingly, we were met with the same from the American Consulate. Precisely because we weren't USIA, we were likewise out of the loop. Throughout the six months, we only met the Cultural attaché one time, and that was to ask us if we would serve as cat-sitters for a weekend while he and his wife were away on a holiday. The man wouldn't even provide us with the Embassy chauffeur, so we were forced to carry our bags the distance: three S-Bahn changes and the long walk from the station to his house along Embassy row in Pankow.

Thank heavens for the Marines attached to the Embassy! Family men themselves, upon meeting us, they didn't hesitate to invite us to the Friday afternoon consulate happy hour, only to be greeted by Peter, the assistant to the cultural attaché and our liaison: "What are YOU doing here." Begrudgingly, we were allowed entry, but that was the last time we attended a Friday get-together as a family. Still, the Marines were good to us, to our boy especially. It was through their invitations that Eric could enjoy satellite telecasts of the Lakers play-offs that spring. And also Marie, the Embassy's librarian, frustrated with her job and put upon, by the rag-tag bunch that called themselves diplomats. French Marie, too, was caught between two worlds.

HAUSFRAU

Journal Entry: Sunday, January 31, 1988

Last week, our American neighbor, Liz, took me to the Kaufhalle. We walked up and down aisles, getting in the way of old lady Germans, Liz explaining patiently, yet hurriedly, me scribbling and shopping and of course panicking at the thought of the inevitable encounter with the checker. Then we come home to discover that the washer doesn't work, after I have loaded it with towels and whites. Then I prepare dinner- a meat loaf – my first and with DDR meat. The oven is broken and I must now panfry meatloaf as hamburger. (And we were w/o lights for 1 ½ days. Later learned about the fuse box.) But their ground beef is lean with very little fat so little, that I keep adding water to the pan. [I hadn't yet figured out that outside the US, you actually mix the meat with the fat!] The day has been a disaster.

So I do a Celeste and in the middle of hamburger frying with water, I throw up. For me to throw up into a German toilet is to seriously be sick.

The next day is better because I do what I am capable of. I scrub the kitchen floor thoroughly and I understand that I've accomplished a task to my satisfaction. A new washer is brought; but it doesn't work. However, after several hours I wonder if it could be a fuse, so Frank and I work the fuses together. The funny washer is fixed and by day's end, I've managed 2 loads of wash. I even made homemade chicken soup for dinner.

I believe that is how we all cope with our new life. As long as you can control something – anything – you grasp onto this place and share in it. Frank mastered the S-Bahn system. He takes to Eric's school, downtown to "Alex," the University, last Sunday to the National History Museum. And he brings us home again. Frank is "S-Bahn Man."

Eric hasn't found his niche yet. Perhaps it's because he must realize that a place can't be found, it must be made for oneself, by oneself. I think I try too hard to make him happy. I must back off. He already knows that language is his barrier and that learning the German language will free him.

January 16, 1988: Food Inventory for Our Trip

1 Italian salami
1 cheddar cheese, 10 oz.
Mini "Babybel" cheeses, 3 ¾ oz.
2 boxes crackers
1 box Twinkies
1 box Cream of Wheat instant packets
1 bag popcorn
1 lb. bag Brach candies
3 packets Oatmeal individual servings
10 envelopes Lipton's soup mix
1 3 oz. grape jelly
2 packs gum
Measuring cups
Measuring spoons
Spices: thyme; cinnamon; oregano; white pepper; ground mustard; garlic salt; sweet basil
2 jars peanut butter, chunky
Betty Crocker Cookbook
California Fresh Cookbook, Junior League of Oakland-East Bay

The staples I'd packed allowed us the buffer we would need for the first days after we were deposited in Marzahn. Meantime, I didn't need the USIA guidebook to explain to me how things would work supermarket-wise in the Eastern Bloc. I would come to regard grocery shopping in the little *Kaufhalle* like shopping back home in a California camp-store: staples and just enough to get by. (And one of everything, the same brand being "government-issue. About as interesting as Springfield canned vegetables in the independent markets back home.) But there was also the same affection we hold for any vacation store beside a campground, including the comraderie toward the other "campers," rushing to see if there was a new delivery of *schnitzel-fleisch*; women together, bumping the little shopping carts in our rush over to the other hausfraus – See them? Milling about by the jarred green beans. (*Russian strawberry jam? Polish pickles? FRESH TOMATOES? My neighbor just pounded on our door, there's a delivery of actual fresh tomatoes! I wonder, did Frank notice the crowd when he left 2 minutes ago to pick up a bottle of Berliner Pilsener? Quick, Eric, run after him.... Too late.... And there is the classic distinction between how men shop and women.*)

My two cookbooks from home, *Betty Crocker* and *California Fresh*, were packed with those challenges in mind. Given the ever-present food shortages, working within the seasons, I still somehow maintained an American, uniquely *California* style, cuisine for my family, and gradually as we made friends, among the Germans, too. Glasnost in the Kitchen. Mid-winter in the upper latitudes of Eastern Europe did pose its challenges for Betty and me both. Fruit salad meant apples. Then the odd-shaped carrots and potatoes, somehow grown on the frozen soil along the western stretch of the Russian plains. And happily always plentiful, what I soon came to call – with affection – "the people's bread". A seedless, sour rye. Actually rather wonderful, as if I had stepped back into time! A world before the American supermarket, when vegetables were jarred, not canned. (Glass is plentiful, tin not.) When one could anticipate the arrival of spring: for among other things, it meant you'd see strawberries and then enjoy asparagus soup with Adelheid at the little café in Prenzlauer Berg.

Meat? Minimal variations of pork cuts (*Schnitzel-Fleisch*); for fall back, hamburger (*Schabbe-Fleisch*," literally "shredded flesh"). To be precise, *schabbe fleisch* with a quarter kilo of *fette*. (I had never known that ground beef was actually beef ground together with fat.) In Berlin, you mixed the fat with the beef – too close to the cow for me! And a lesson for me in language: German is a language of precision in thought. What you say the thing is, *is* what it is. This precision, of course, translated into the everyday. There was never any dilly-dallying with German.

But I also imagined that the East Germans would be curious about *our* cooking. *California Fresh* included beautiful drawings, as did the color photographs in *Betty Crocker*. We soon learned that the Germans had a deep appreciation for quality bookbinding, including photographs. I'd always appreciated food photography, but never more so than when

I'd observe how the East Germans perceived the color graphite drawing of squid on a cutting board, from the Junior League cookbook. Or at Humboldt University when Frank presented the graduate students with 100 copies of the Norton American Literature. (I remember that fifty *Great Gatsby* texts left no impression on them, whatsoever. It didn't make sense.) I taught them to make salads without lettuce – never saw a head the entire time we lived there – and also without cabbage, a staple at every German meal. Together, we'd make Italian dressing, substituting the always plentiful sunflower oil for olive oil. Unfortunately, the two-way street wasn't exactly what one would hope. I learned to eat brown bread with *schmaltz*: lard, seasoned heavily with paprika. Yet and still, lard.

I quickly learned, though, that what the *Kaufhalle* lacked in variety and on demand accessibility – strawberries year-round; avocadoes from Chile – was compensated for in a true socialist philosophy about food distribution itself. No one went hungry in Berlin. All the staples were not only available, but they were cheap. Cheap, as in government-subsidized. And, it was organic although the Germans wouldn't have seen it that way. With limited access to petroleum resources, fertilizers and pesticides were low on the list for allocations, top being defense. Vegetables were grown organically, fed with the manure from the chickens and pigs on the large farms. In turn, the pigs were fed from the vegetable scraps every household collected and daily deposited in the designated garbage can below in the basement area. To be sure, no kitchen was supplied with a garbage disposal.

One week after we arrived in Marzahn, I watched my first Prime Time GDR broadcast on the – what else – black and white television. The evening telecast devoted itself to the *Kartoffel* – Potato. The most amazing part of the show, and it truly amazed me, was the recipe for their version of the stuffed bell pepper -- but without the bell pepper -- and with two variations. The first involved a watermelon baller and a large yellow onion. After hollowing out the onion, the chef stuffed it with mashed potatoes, set an onion "cap" on top, brushed with melted butter, and then placed the onion onto a baking dish. The second variation presented a hollowed out potato this time, then stuffed with over-cooked mush, Brussel sprouts. Both were baked in the oven several minutes, until browned on top.

That single cooking episode argued sufficiently against government-controlled television. Basically, the GDR, through its two chefs, manipulated for more potato consumption -- ditto that – less disgruntled potato consumers. That's the stuff that got inside me even more than the police surveillance. Surveillance comes from *without*. You can sense it, feel it, at times see it in the student designated to spy on the others in Frank's Friday afternoon class. You return home from shopping. After several hours away, the coal dust has already settled again after the morning's sweeping, and there are the shoe prints. Stasi have been here again, searching about for who knows what.

But the potato broadcasts work their way *into* you, until finally by God, they do look good, mush and all. Buttered onion cap! Or worse, they don't look anything at all but what you expect to see. And by that point, you have no opinion at all.

But my frustration with the *Kaufhalle* was also balanced in another respect. I would feel good about shopping, knowing that my footprint was small, sized the same as my neighbors in the apartment building, throughout East Berlin, and across the GDR. (Yes, there were the party members. Same as our own pols at home. With power, privilege. . . .) I was limited to two choices of cooking oil. *Sonnenblumen* (Sunflower) and another that had the look of the used oil I'd collect from my frying pan back home. All the vegetables were limited to those available in northern wintry clime: potatoes, cabbages, leeks, and onions. On the other hand, a half dozen varieties of ketchup, including one Curry-flavored. Mackerel-Hoppen, likewise. Cheap and plentiful, the construction workers would purchase cans of fish for their break times in mid-morning. And then there is something about breaking open a chicken egg only to notice that bit of poop on the white shell. You are reminded where exactly eggs come from!

But that first week in our *Neue-Baue* flat! I hadn't counted on how one communicates across the currency problem. Like just about everything in the East, currency was complicated. About as serious as it got. Theirs was "soft currency"; the West German Mark and US Dollar, "hard." Officially and on our side of the border, the currency exchange for East and West marks was one for one. But unofficially and absolutely in the West, about 15 Ost-Marks to 1 Deustche Mark.

This meant that we could rarely pay with western currency, an expectation that Americans had long since been accustomed to. The exception the GDR banks and the Inter-Stores, state-operated stores with western goods where only western currency was accepted, and on the one-to-one exchange. But both bank and inter-store were situated in downtown Berlin, a good train ride from suburban Marzahn. So what do you do when you arrive in a country on the weekend, no ATM, and peer into an empty larder? What do you do when the Humboldt University student who delivered us from Tegel to our flat – on the way, only one fleeting stop at the East German Cultural Exchange Office near Alexanderplatz – and then leaves us with nothing except three S-Bahn tickets for the next day? First, you open up the Care Package from home and feed your family Lipton's boxed chicken noodle soup, with Babybel cheese and crackers.

Then you make your way to the *Kaufhalle* in the building nearby. Luckily, an American graduate student was our next-door neighbor. Liz had lent me a few Ost-Marks and small coins to get us through. I trekked to the little market – *Kaufhalles* are all little, about the size of a 7/11 and not as interesting. After I had made my way to the register, I took out a twenty and unthinkingly handed it over to a clerk who at first, gave no reaction. Just sober-faced. Then again. Silence. Silence all around me. The checker and the women in line clearly expressing their discomfort as all now did their best to distance themselves from the American. Understandable, too. In a country in which it was later revealed that 25% of the population was employed as *Stasi*, one could correctly imagine that one or two of those fellows were stationed about. The other customers knew this; so did my checker. Stupidly, I didn't.

At this point, the checker starts in, all in German. I was certain solely in the imperative tense. On and on, screeching at me, her decibel level higher and higher. The sounds so replicated the pitch level of a squawking chicken that I'd have done *anything* to end it. Stop it!

I opened my wallet, spilling out every East German coin Liz had given me several Ost-Marks and various smaller coins, including the lightweight phennigs. She could have her pick. I didn't care, take it all. I wanted away from the bwark-bwarking aimed directly at me. Suddenly, the screeching stopped, mid-sentence. She picked her way through the coins, counting in her head. Then she plucked them in the register, and we were done. She was done with me!

Actually, I have that clerk to thank pretty much for saving my life a few days later – mine and Eric's. The first two weeks, Frank and I would share chauffeur duties taking Eric to his school in East Berlin: a good 40-minute one-way trip, including the 15 minute walk from our flat to the Marzahn subway station. I'd take Eric in the morning, then schlep my way home again; Frank would be there to bring him home in the afternoon. At the end of two weeks exactly, Eric was now on his own. He was a city kid, for Frank, it didn't matter where the city was, either. On this particular morning, I was frazzled; the stove wasn't working again, Eric was dawdling, we had left late, and I wasn't thinking too clearly as I exited **one stop too soon**. In East Berlin, once you leave the train, you've forfeited your remaining ride. To hop back on, even seconds later, was a serious offense. Serious enough that even the doofusses at the Embassy thought enough to warn us in advance. I realized my mistake even before I popped my head up the top of the stairwell and saw that we had stepped off one station too soon. Quick! We raced back to catch the train which hadn't yet left the platform, that's how quick we were, up the stairs and back.

But just before we stepped off the platform, a subway controller had planted himself between the train door and us. Again, that jabbering in German, but I got the gist of it right off. All policemen speak the same international language. I was pretty certain that he wouldn't let me off with a warning; more likely, I was about to be arrested. (I can't say as I blame the East Berliners. Mass transit was cheap there, among the many basic services heavily subsidized. A simple fare without transfer was under 20 phennigs.) Meantime, the controller is going on and on in German, no good outcome for me. No way for me to telephone or even telegraph Frank, Humboldt University, the American Consulate. (And what exactly would the Assistant Cultural Attache, Peter Claussen, do for me? I considered that, too, and found no comfort.) My boy's hand tightened on mine, or was it mine on Eric's? All I could think at that time was this was it. I was about to be arrested. This was the *Stasi* body search I had feared. And what about my kid? How do I let Frank, let the Consulate, *know*?

Then I remembered my *Kaufhalle* chicken lady. I didn't even think, it was pure instinctive push back – the German checker and her squawking. If I had found her screeching so intolerable that I would do anything to get away, well maybe. . . So I located just the right decibel level, a high-pitched screeching to match hers, only this in American English. "I'm an American – We're going to School – Schule! Schule! Kinder! -- I'm a mother – I'm an American –I missed my train – This is my kid -----"

And then, he waved us off.

Chicken Lady Politics.

THE JEWISH QUESTION

Journal Entry: Monday, April 11, 1988

Back home from our weekend in Thalhaim. And as usual for life in the DDR, the time there was contradictory in nature. . . . The trip down we shared our cabin with a man in his mid-forties I would guess. He works as a design engineer, designer of fabrics for trains and workplaces, I think, and he was returning to his home in Karl-Marx Stadt.

Of course he wanted to speak with the Americans – that would be Frank – because the man spoke no English. Speaking to us allows these people to voice their anguishes in a way not possible within their Gemeinschaft. It's a chance to whisper beyond their walls, I think.

I asked him, via Frank, if Germans were embittered over the division: toward the Nazis, toward the Allied Powers. The textile engineer answered in three parts: "First, Germany lost the war. That is a fact. Second, it was right that we lost the war." (He knew the number, the six million.) "Third . . . the world remembers what Germany did, and Germans remember as well, every day. It is never out of their minds."

***

But while the German people clearly do remember, how well do they grasp what they were responsible for? During our time in East Berlin, I came to understand that the two Germanys, East and West, confronted their racial remembrance in such different ways; but then again, was it so different? In the DDR, the Russians ensured that the memories of the war be kept alive. Throughout

East Berlin were the war memorials to the Russian soldier as well as statues of Lenin in every section of the city. (Lenin having recently supplanted Stalin statuary.)

But then would come the question central to all Germans. The central question of responsibility directed toward the heart of a people's conscience, and they would side-step. "We are Communists, not Fascists." Them, not us. *They.*

In 1988, the city statistics reported that 200 Jews remained in Berlin, DDR. Early in our stay we took the S-Bahn to visit the old Jewish cemetery in East Berlin, among our first outings. I recall that it was bitter cold. A landlocked city, Berlin stands at the western end of a thousands' miles stretch of the Russian plain. The winds whip miles across through winter, seemingly gaining in intensity as they move westward. The graveyard's barren trees and shrubs are nearly indistinguishable from the broken tombstones scattered about. This had been a cemetery for the Berlin elite, evidenced by the ornate sculptures. Aside from the two or three caretakers, we walked the cemetery grounds alone that February day. Even in the mess of it all, I could see that the sleeping shrubs were pruned; a bit farther off, I observed a woman attending to the lower branches of a tree. The dozens of destroyed stones had been left undisturbed and as they had fallen fifty years ago, a remembrance of another winter's day, November 9, 1938. *Kristellnacht.*

The sign on the wall outside the entrance reads: "Silence." I don't believe we'd have needed the sign at all, though. The three of us were each lost in our own thoughts, reflecting on the deeply-rooted hatred that sought to obliterate an entire people, even in the grave. You step through and it's as though you are stepping simultaneously into and outside of the city, walled out by time itself. The wintry barrenness of the trees and shrubs on that February Sunday replicated what would have greeted the *Hitler-Jugen* decades previous.

To the right, I noted five more people tilling the frozen earth, cutting back the winter-dead shrubbery in preparation for spring. We were the only other visitors that day, and like the caretakers, we stepped gingerly over the stones that lay about. The winds from the East cut threw me, matching the icy coldness inside me as I reflected on the mindset of ordinary Berliners in 1938. I understood why the 200 who remained would leave this cemetery as it was after the Night of Broken Glass. Is the Jewish Cemetery still unchanged, I wonder?

Two months later, we visited Sachsenhausen, Berlin's concentration camp. I had been postponing a visit to a death camp, even though every German we met had insisted upon. Never any mention of Martin Luther's famous proclamation in Erfurt. Nor the suggestion to take the train for a day-trip to historical Potsdam or even charming Kopernick along the Spree. But to a person – Frank's colleagues and students at Humboldt, my German girlfriends, even the occasional stranger with whom we'd strike up a conversation – Berliners would urge us to visit Buchenwald, East Germany's most infamous death camp and the one to which every schoolchild was required to visit.

I finally resigned myself, but not to appease the Germans. I opted instead to take Eric to nearby Sachsenhausen, on the other side of Berlin from Marzahn. My son's father is Jewish, and his son had the right to stand there and see it for himself. In fact, with the *Intifada*, Frank and I understood Eric's particular vulnerability to the rising anti-Semitism in 1988. As a precaution, we'd changed his last name for the passport, from his father's "Friedman" to Frank's Anglo-Saxon "McConnell." In 1988, as now, international travel posed risk. Leon Klinghoffer was not yet a distant memory. Just before Christmas in 1988, Pan Am Flight 103 was blown up over Lockerbie, Scotland. The same flight route that we had taken home in late summer.

Just as the 1936 Summer Olympics were underway in Berlin, con-struction of Sachsenhausen Concentration Camp neared completion just a few miles distant from the athletic competitions. The trek out there was an easy day's excursion for Eric and me. We took the S-Bahn to Oranienburg, across Berlin from our Marzahn suburb. Upon disembark-ing, we were surprised that there was no signage indicating the prox-imity of the camp. We walked the one block up from the station. Then a sharp right turn along a tree-lined street. I noticed the lovely homes, clearly post-war. Early springtime, the flowers were now beginning to bloom. Another German paradox: We witnessed the preparations for the new season, its promise of life, as we walked the remaining stretch to Sachsenhausen camp.

One block more and the camp entrance looms suddenly. Much of the old camp is gone, but a good portion, an open space the size of a football field, was still in use, now by the military. Even at age ten, the irony wasn't lost on Eric as together we observed the soldiers goose-stepping in formation on the parade grounds. We first walked through the camp's main building, where the museum was housed. Among the various displays, Eric discovered an electronic mapping of Nazi-occupied Europe, clearly designed as a teaching tool for schoolchildren. Eric pushes the first button and the famous camps (Auschwitz, Buchenwald, Dachau . . .) light up. He pushes the next button, this for the medium-sized camps like Sachsenhausen (200,000 inmates; 100,000 killed). Then the last, the small labor camps adjoined like appendages to villages throughout Eastern Europe. All of Europe lit up before us.

Once outside and free to walk about, we saw that the killing pit was still intact. At first, the Nazis practiced execution by firing squad. Later, they were to craft a four-fold mechanical gallows: ". . . a foot box held the feet firmly, and the victim was not hanged – he was cruelly torn apart." Instead of free-falling through an opening, this noose was intended to pull its victim upward, similar to the medieval drawn and quartered. The execution square was deep enough that we couldn't peer out to the grounds beyond.

Next, we walked to the barracks. On our way, we peered inside the humiliating public latrines. Then, stepped inside the Jewish barracks, standing together as my boy pointed and counted out each of the bunks, stacked atop one another and reaching to the ceiling: "One, two, three . . . forty-two, forty-three. . ." Back outside again, we made our way to the medical building, still sparkling clean, and as I imagined it would have been maintained forty years earlier. Likewise, the basement was beautifully tiled. We looked to the basement front and its shoot from outside and above, where the bodies would have been pushed to storage below ad stacked, later to be examined by the "doctors" in the laboratory above. The exam rooms looked not much different from those of Eric's pediatrician at the clinic back home.

The first page of the Sachsenhausen National Memorial reads in its English translation:

"In deep respect we bow down here before our beloved dead who fought against war, fascism and militarism, who were the victims of Nazi terror. This place is dedicated to their memory: to the memory of the countless martyrs and heroes of the antifascist resistance, as a reminder to our generation and those to follow that never again must fascist and militarist barbarity be allowed to sweep over our people or over other peoples. . . . Here they were hounded and tormented to death, tortured and butchered only because they loved their people, only because they loved freedom and democracy more than their own lives, because they were socialists. . . ."

Where is reference to the Jews? Where any mention of German responsibility?

WE aren't responsible. It was the Fascists, those on the other side of the Wall. WE, along with our Soviet comrades, WE were the true victims. I recall the great scene from the film, *Judgment at Nuremburg*: First, the tired refrain -- "Nobody knew!" Then the prosecuting attorney's reply: "Don't you know that it was the Eskimos who invaded Germany and took over. That's how those terrible things happened. It wasn't the fault of the Germans. It was those damned Eskimos."

When the three of us returned to Berlin in June, 1990, the first thing we noticed was the graffito on the former eastern side. There in red paint at the entry to an S-Bahn station: the swastika. Eskimos.

LETTERS FROM HOME

1988 doesn't seem so long ago in retrospect. In many ways, it's as though it were last week. Fifteen years after the Goleta Costco opened, I still feel strange behind the over-sized shopping cart, memories rush back of my Marzahn *Kaufhalle*, and limited by what I could manage in two cloth shopping bags. (I still feel the pressure in my right arm occasionally!) But now, as I read through the letters from home again, 25 years may as well have been 25 centuries, such the quantum transformation in global communications since. Back then, there was no Internet for email forwards. *Can you imagine what we were spared?* No email forwards of goofy platitudes on friendship or Obama birth theories from AM radio enthusiasts. No i-phones or blue-tooth devices, either; and then, the obnoxious Skype! In fact, we didn't even have telephone access, private or public, in the apartment building, let alone our flat. We lived like the majority of East German citizenry, communicating through letter or telegram. (Ah! For the spontaneity of the visitor just arriving unannounced at our door. Last week, it took 3 emails to and fro to arrange a simple luncheon date with pal, Carolyn. It seemed the most natural thing to have Adelheid or our fellow Fulbrighter, David Robinson, arrive unannounced, on the chance that we might be home!) And on the rare occasion when I did need to phone home to the States pronto, I would dedicate the full day for travel by S-Bahn to West Berlin's main train station, wait in line to use the public phone, and hurriedly talk through what I needed in -- under 3 minutes. Then the two-hour trek back home, waiting in the endless lines at Friedrichstrasse station. . . .

Letters from the States travelled a full 3 weeks before arrival in Marzahn. Packages even more problematic, as everything would have been given the once-over before final arrival to 25 Marzahner Promenade, DDR. But real letters! Relics from a time before email and texting and twittering. "Hard Copy." Single-draft, handwritten *writing* without the aid of Spell-Check, the sole draft imprinting spontaneity, raw feelings. Written on onion paper to keep the weight down.

I wonder what it is like today for fellow Americans, posted about the world and with instant access to home? Is the anticipation lost to them? The waiting for the post: "Will there be a letter for me?" And even before you opened it: scanning the return address – my mother or youngest sister, Patty; my UCSB co-worker, Perry. Joanne Schneider, my PTA partner at Monte Vista School, missing me for our spring teachers appreciation luncheon. Then I would inspect the postage. In 1988, it cost 44 cents to send a letter to Europe. I see that the stamp is a drawing of the left wingspan from a 1935 transpacific plane with a tiny American flag above the cockpit. I would have noticed that detail, too, in 1988. Everything was important in our insulated world behind the Wall.

It never mattered what they wrote to us, either. We really wanted to hear about the mundane, the everyday life that we had left behind. Frank's colleague John Carroll, bemoaning the 97 students in his course, "American Lit after 1917," and the 67 in another class. My sister relating her babysitter problems: the sitter up and left; Mom now comes to watch Kelly and Jaime, complaining about the early hours. Then there was the letter from Mom that prompted one of those treks to the West-Berlin train station for a panicked call home when she described our sublet townhome as having "that lived-in look." What does that mean, "lived-in?" What could the visiting scholar's family from Ireland have managed in a little over a month?

* * *

And those challenges to familial communication in a place without telephones. Eric and I return home late one afternoon to Frank's missive:

Dear Wormy (the correct spelling) –

Read Marxism all morning, wrote fiction all afternoon, drank a little beer, and missed you like ten kinds of sonofabitch.

Am going to spread culture with Keith, I will return immediately hereafter. Great letter from Jon Reed, and unread letter – opened by mistake from Gail, Herb, et, al.

Two beers, for you, chilling in the fridge, plus 500g. of roast beef (no lettuce, no cukes, no Schnitzelfleisch –tut mir led). Back in a jiffy or a taxi or an S-Bahn.

Love you, Gunter V

CHECKPOINT CHARLIE

Lyrics for "Born in the GDR," the E-Strasse Band
(Compliments to Bruce Springsteen)

Had a conference with Helmut Kohl –
Said, "Hey, Daddy, let's a rock n roll."
Organized a thousand Commie cats,
Took 'em all down to Ernst Thalman Platz.
Took the S-Bahn out to Old Marzahn,
Saw the Neu-Bau, said, "What's going on?"
I'm a cool, rockin' Stasi in the GDR.
I'm a cool, cool, rockin' Stasi in the GDR.

Wanna join the Socialist citizenry,
Gotta marry a woman from the SED.
Cruised on down to the US Embassy.
Said to the VoPos – "Hey, Man, don' you mess with me."
Checkpoint Charlie really got me bummed,
Because, hey, the VoPos say that I can't come.
Tried hiding out in the trunk of a car,
Well, they opened that Trabi, said, "Boy, who do you think you are?"
So I'm sitting in jail, doing 1, 2, 3.

Til they think they've re-educated me.
I'm a cool, rockin' Stasi in the GDR.
I'm a cool, cool, rockin' Stasi in the GDR. . .

To have lived in Cold War Berlin is to have been planted in the direct center of the world. Long-range missiles from across the Atlantic, at home in the heartland, and eastward, somewhere in the vast Soviet continent, humming in their silos. Middle-range from NATO posts and Eastern bloc nations. Closer still, the two halves to the city itself, facing off, each eerily familiar from the memory of what was in the before: before the wall, before the allied bombings in the early months of 1945. The face-off across No Man's Land, an expansive field empty except for the occasional squirrel scurrying about. No trees. And then, Checkpoint Charlie itself. The bull's eye, if you will.

Checkpoint Charlie is a point on the map; 52 degrees north latitude by 13 degrees east longitude. Friedrichstrasse between Zimmerstrasse (East) and Mauererstrasse (West). The American kiosk faced across a single paved city block, technically No Man's Land, to the East German border station. But for me walking the stretch, many times alone, Charlie represented more than the border crossing from one city block to another. To have walked across the pavement was to trek from the Eastern half of the world to the Western, the globe divided into two hemispheres. One was absolutely conscious of that fact.

I first knew Checkpoint Charlie from the East, on those occasions when I would venture to West Berlin for shopping and usually without my family. Depending on the lines that day, I could be several hours or the entire day away from Marzahn. The three block walk from the S-Bahn station and as I near closer to the border crossing, the crowds diminish, the last block emptied, even of the little Trabants. The single-story building through which I entered, passing through and out, just under the shadow of the guard tower. I'd chat with the attendant at the counter, usually the same woman, to whom I would declare my business in the West, and about as casually as I would have spoken to a store clerk at home: "What are you shopping for today? A Walkman for your son?" Upon my return, present my purchases or not: "The Walkman was too expensive. Perhaps another day. But I found some marzipan candies for Easter!" She'd open my purse and the various parcels, chatting all the time like old friends. How odd to experience congeniality here!

But, you could never trust it. There was another time when I had taken the other route available to Americans traveling between East and West Berlin: Friedrichstrasse subway station. I had gone to West-Berlin to purchase a cane for Frank, then suffering the gout. Not surprisingly, none were to be found in the East. Upon my return, the station was packed; clearly, I had about an hour wait to make it through the line. I tried my best to manage my other parcels in my right arm, as I leaned my left onto Frank's new cane. Next thing, a young German border guard arrives, instructing me to follow him. Of course, no one else says a word, they are frozen where they stand. I pretend not to understand. He returns a few minutes later. Same schpiel, and he beckons me out of there. I don't say a word. As he returns yet again, I finally get it. The pimply-faced young soldier thinks I'm lame! He's trying to do the right thing. So now I have a new problem, even worse in my mind. How to feign lameness in order to make it across! The whole point of moving across the border, was to be as inconspicuous as possible. To be invisible.

Perched atop the guard tower at Checkpoint Charlie, other young East German soldiers notable for the machine guns that didn't quite match their pimply faces and ill-fitting uniforms. I'd walk along and look up. Then back at the U.S. soldiers in the American kiosk, he was watching me, too. Watching out.

Charlie was a place apart. Most for its silence in the midst of a city capital and the West's cosmopolitan centerpiece. It's the silence that stays with me these years after. As if I were asleep still, in a dream. In the midst of a bustling city, the unnerving effect on time itself which appeared to slow down just as time sputters the instant before a car collision.

I remember the quiet. I walk across and see the construction workers just beyond the American kiosk. But I don't hear them. Nor the cars. Nor the sounds of people gawking at us, *at me*, across in the East. So quiet, I am conscious of my breath. I'd reflect on where I was, the center of the political world and all its energies poised at me. The palatable collision of two worlds and one city block poised between: Charlie and me.

I recall, too, being keenly sensitive to nature about me. How could the same sun shine here, as it did in the Tiergarten? Later in springtime, the birds had returned and they would fly over the fields to my left, No Man's

Land, but it didn't exist for them. No borders for the grasses, nor for the spring pollen carried in the winds.

I recall another time, when we picnicked in Pankow's lovely city park late in April. The weekend of housesitting for the Cultural Attache in Embassy Row, located in the fashionable district in East Berlin, so close to the border. On that day, Eric and I decided to explore the park a bit. We left Frank on the blanket to read the Christa Wolf novel he'd been given by his department chair, Mueller.

Nearby, a tiny stream! Imagining ourselves European explorers wandering the Nile upstream to its source, we did same with our brook. It meandered through the grass, then a turn to the woods just ahead. Then just a split second after I considered the mesh fencing in the stream, I looked up and straight ahead. Fifty feet ahead was the border. I saw its eyes first. The guard's German shepherd was intent on us, thankfully on the other side of a metal fence. But those eyes? The animal's eyes never wavered as we stood, frozen, like prey. We were prey.

And yet precisely because Berlin was situated smack in the middle of the world, there was this fellowship that one could feel among the people who lived there. Even toward strangers. Among my best memories of that time and place, the streetcar ride I shared with an old Russian woman. The day before, Eric's class had taken a field trip into the center of East Berlin. While out, he noticed a queue forming outside a store. He didn't see what it was exactly that was in supply, but that wouldn't have mattered. It was bound to be something scarce and wonderful, and so, in demand. The next day, I set myself to the task! (You wouldn't think twice about setting aside a day – hour in / hour back and who knows how long in the line – to purchase something, anything that wasn't a potato or pork. This particular day, I returned home with two jars of Polish pickles, and Eric was thrilled!)

I'd picked up a streetcar and plopped myself down next to an old woman, so wrinkled she had that special aura peculiar to the aged. Her own beauty. Americans were rare in East Berlin those days, and I clearly interested her. She initiated the conversation – in Russian! I'd reply in my pigeon German, but giving it up for English. Somehow, though, during those minutes together on the tram, we actually understood one another. Two women, one old and the other young, but talking womanish things.

She in her Russian, me responding clumsily, to be sure, but in English. And yet, we clicked!

I eventually figured out that she was visiting from Moscow. That she liked Stalin. (Her peasant family had survived on Stalin's bread.) And by the way, did I happen to know where the Soviet Embassy was? Would I take her? My entire life I had grown up in dread of communist global incursion. I remembered it from my *Weekly Readers*. The regularly scheduled "Duck and Cover" drills throughout grade school. And she was asking me to take her to the Soviet Union's embassy!

Of course I knew and beckoned her to follow me off the tram. I knew the place, everyone did who traveled about Berlin. You couldn't miss it. The Soviet Embassy commanded a full block along Unter den Linden, near Potsdamer Platz, the heart of the city. A stark gray-stoned edifice walled in all around with a statue of Lenin in the small garden near the entry. Certainly on a grander scale than the modest American Embassy on a side-street several blocks away. (I would always be surprised when I'd be walking along Unter den Linden and suddenly look left – halfway down the block, there was our flag. My heart would stir. My country!)

The Polish pickles could wait a bit more. I escorted the woman off the tram. Together we walked the remaining block to the Soviet Embassy, as though we were neighbors out for an afternoon stroll together. Once there, I felt like Tin Man peering over to the Wicked Witch's stone castle. About as intimidating, too. There was this tiny window in the door – like a tiny door carved into the door. I rang the bell and the barely visible face appeared behind the window. Next thing, she is summoned in and the door – both doors, little and big -- quickly closed, emphatically closed, on me. And yet that memory of her remains among my sweetest of Berlin.

It seems now and looking back to that year, that our family lived the entire time in No Man's Land. It wasn't necessary to give it the name: Checkpoint Charlie or Friedrichstrasse Station. We were separate, not actually ever part of any place. The State Department had abandoned us to our own devices throughout. Humboldt University faculty and students couldn't risk meeting with us outside Frank's classroom, only when it was official. Frank's birthday party. The May Day parade. Our small American community of Fulbrighters – Ann and her husband, Ralph, sweet Liz down the hall, David Robinson, the only one among us with a computer and therefore, the one most likely to be subject to searches.

And our Adelheid, along with her flotilla of friends: Heike Schneider, Tanya the Russian, and sweet Gerlinde (Sweet Sale, now gone, too). Adelheid, the one German we met -- heck, the one person German or American posted there -- who was clearly her own person. How she survived a free, authentic spirit, not caring who or where, I'll never quite fathom. Adelheid Wedel, like Berlin, remains an enigma.

POSTSCRIPT

Twenty-five years ago, Frank and I sat riveted to the television set that night in early November. ABC's Peter Jennings was giving continuous coverage as we watched – stunned – to see what would have been inconceivable just 18 months earlier. People, some of them Berliners we had known, climbing up and over the Wall. *Die Wende*, the Turn. We telephoned Adelheid straightaway, then impulsively invited her family to visit us in California over Christmas. They came, and we went, where else, but Disneyland!

But throughout that night in November, 1989, the two of us huddled together in worry. It was too fast! They weren't prepared. They wouldn't understand that Capitalism doesn't provide the safety nets that Socialism had set in place. They couldn't see that the West Berliners' free donuts and coffee would get old pretty quick – as it did. Or that the rents would rise. No more *Kindergelt*. No more guaranteed jobs. And what would happen to the pensioners?

And then we considered the Boogey Man. For so long, the enemy had been the face of the Soviet empire. Who now would replace it, we wondered. We had no doubt that the boogey would be replaced, the question was simply, "Who?" We were given our answer twelve years later, Frank already gone two of those years. Like all Americans, I remember the September morning that I awoke to breaking news, a plane had flown into the World Trade Center. And then a second. The name, Osama bin Laden, the new boogey.

FRANK

"Sergeant Carmen Walker, bringing you home . . . On the Edge!"

(From the UC, Santa Barbara *Daily Nexus*, January 12, 1989: "BEST IN MUSIC FOR 1988")

Since I spent most of 1988 teaching in Berlin, Haupstadt der D.D. R. ("East Berlin" to George Bush and his kind), I had, shall we say, limited access to what was happening in American rock and roll. Not till I got back did I find out from my students here and from Rolling Stone that heavy metal is to be taken seriously, that the Boss has lost it and is now just the CEO, that U2 is as overrated as Kahlil Gibran used to be, and that Michael Jackson has made the difficult transition from weird talent to weird nerd. But hell, I suspected all that before I left.

*So thank God for AFN, American Forces Radio (not "Armed Forces Radio" – we don't **say** things like that anymore) which we could pick up from Berlin-West. Now AFN is like going back to the '50s, the real seedtime of rock, which is to say **my** generation, right? Like, the DJ's patter never, never rises out of junior high humor: these guys make the KTYD jocks sound like George Will. And nobody makes solemn distinctions among "new wave," "pop," "metal," "rap," or whatever. It's all, you know, like – music (remember that Elvis' early idol, lord love him, was Dean Martin). And, most important, the elementary unit of rock in the AFN timewarp is the **single**. How refreshing to be reminded that, before the Beatles, the Kinks, and the Who invented that loose and baggy monster, the "concept album," an album was just that – an album, as in "photo album," a collection of singles if you had the money to buy them all at once ($3.98 as opposed to 35 cents – yes, really, those were the prices of my youth).*

So: Based on an admittedly skewed and delightful sojourn in Haupstadt, here, for what they are worth, are my picks for fave raves of the year.

1. **Rick Astley,** *"Never Gonna Give You Up." Has to be tops, because, as my wife says, it's the best bar song since "Proud Mary." We used to fantasize about GIs boogeying to this with various and sundry Ulrikes, Ingrids and Katrinas – or, for that matter, Jurgens, Erichs and Gottfrieds.*

2. **George Harrison,** *"When We Was Fab." Almost as much as "Heading for the Light" from the Wilburys album, a dead-on recreation of the Beatles sound in all its glorious silliness. Harrison, like Entwhistle of the Who, turns out to be the faithful keeper of his group's flame.*

3. **Pebbles,** *"Girl Friend." Why the hell not? She sings better than Tiffany, has more soul than five Whitneys, and the song is a beautiful recreation of high school crisis, which, after all, is where rock begins and ends.*

4. **Tiffany,** *Anything because it all sounds the same. So did Brill Building pop, and if you think being mass-marketed stops it from being great rock and roll, you've become too sophisticated – or not sophisticated enough.*

5. **George Michael,** *"Father Figure." If Roy Orbison was the Caruso of rock, brother George is its Sinatra, or, better, its Mel Torme. He's got miles and miles of chops, and he knows exactly what he's doing.*

I'm not sure Robert Hilburn would agree with this list. But whenever I hear any of those songs, I know that part of me will always us find itself back under a grey rainy sky in a city I love. And if that's not what music is for, what in the world is it for?

Frank McConnell, Department of English

REPORT FROM GERMANY

SOMETHING GAINED & LOST
What Unification Feels Like

(Published in *Commonweal*: October 26, 1990)
Frank McConnell

"How thick is the Wall, Frank?"

That was the first question a friend asked me when I got back, in 1988, from six months teaching at Humboldt University in East Berlin. I thought it was a pretty silly question at the time. I know better now.

After half-a-year living and working in one of the most rigorously monitored of socialist states, I was, like all half-cocked travelers, brimming with insights to amaze and impress my stay-at-home pals. Like: The GDR ran on systematized paranoia- the infamous *Stasi*, or Secret Police – that would have made Orwell or Kafka look for another line of work. And like: Despite this, some things about the system were – well, dammit, *good*. People managed to live as happily and warmly, it seemed to us, as they did in the States. My *parteilich* friends – Party members – seemed seriously devoted to socialism, to working for a vision of universal good will (and *we* make Donald Trump a media icon.) When I jokingly told a Berlin colleague of mine, Horst, that my Catholic background would probably keep me out of the Party, he said gravely – Horst is a grave fellow – "Oh, no, Frank. We wouldn't admit you because you think everything's a joke."

These, and many more, were among the *dicta* I was all set to launch at the drop of an *obiter*. And what did I get? "How thick is the Wall?" is what I got.

Then came November 1989, and suddenly the Wall wasn't thick at all. Gloria Steinem called it the first feminine revolution, because there was no bloodshed and then everybody went shopping. George Will, on national TV, intoned that "the spirit of Thomas Jefferson is abroad in the world" – ever see a conservative on speed? And, as they sing in *Carousel*, it was a real nice clambake, and we all had a real good time.

I did get a Christmas card from Horst. I quote: "We are of course glad that many corruptions, like the *Stasi*, are gone. Still, Frank, I can't help feeling that one of mankind's dreams has died." I did not think it was a joke.

So when my wife and I were invited to return to Humboldt this August to teach a crash course in "American Speech and Culture," it was – for me at least – a little like planning a date with the girl you took to the prom in '68. You keep telling yourself how great it'll be, after all this time. And telling yourself. We knew that problems had already set in: epidemic unemployment, a nightmare currency regularization, the massive failure of GDR industry to compete. But there's knowing, and then there's knowing.

The fact is, we missed the party, but we got there for the hangover.

Our first lesson in the thickness of the Wall was the drive from Tegel Airport in the West to our apartment in the East. *Berlin Haupstadt der GDR,* Berlin the Capital City of the GDR – that was how every map, roadsign, and even matchbox referred to the place, and it was silly and brave. Despite its shabbiness, its exploitation by the USSR, and its annual fight against bankruptcy, it kept insisting that it was the *Hauptstadt* and, somehow, people believed: that it *was* a city, not "East Berlin" but *Berlin Hauptstadt*. Act as if you have faith, says Augustine, and faith will come.

But now the Wall was down, reunification was, as the Stones say, just a kiss away, and we were driving through West Berlin's Kurfursteindam – Vegas with sausages- into the grey buildings and tiny shops that we, too, had thought of as a city. But it wasn't a *Hauptstadt* or even a *Stadt* anymore. It was just the poor part of town.

Our teaching gig was supposed to be for three weeks. We quit after four days, left Berlin four days later. (Four days after *that* the coalition government collapsed, but I fear we can't take credit.) We quit because we, and our students, were being scammed. They were forty, middle-aged teachers of high-school Russian. There are about 160,000 of them in the GDR. There are about 6,000 teachers of high school English. All that, of course, has to change now. So unless our students, whose English was not rusty but rusted, could pass, *by September,* a competency exam in English, they would be – to use one English word everybody in the GDR knows these days – sacked. Our high falutin' course in American Culture (tapes, videos, etc.) had been sold to *them* as a last chance to learn enough about irregular verbs to keep off the street. But on the third day of our class Bonn announced that in February 1991 it would be sending in 1,000 teachers of English to East Berlin to "fill the need." Is there such a concept as kitchen colonialism?

The day my wife, Celeste, and I told them we were quitting, and why, half were angry and half, worse, were in tears; not because we were the Fred and Ginger of teaching, but because they knew this was it. I had become pretty friendly with one guy named Klaus. The last day we stood in the hall and chatted. "We know about what will happen, *nothing,*" he said. "They tell us, and what can we say? I don't' know. My wife is sacked, my son is sacked, and -- maybe I sell insurance, ja?"

The sadness gets more complicated, though. (I think the central fact about Berlin, of all cities, is that nothing to do with it is *ever* simple.) These folks were frightened and confused -- because *their wish came true.* Sure, Berlin felt like a *Hauptstadt.* But, sure, too, just across the Wall, was West Berlin, brimming with *stuff* and seductive as all hell. Every junkie knows the routine: hey, wouldn't you like to try it *once?* And every junkie knows that "once" is not a real word. Not in the junk lexicon.

"I feel like I'm in prison!" had exclaimed our friend, A., about the Wall in '88. A. had a lovely flat in the center of town and a prestigious job as editor of Berlin's best arts and letters weekly. Now she will very likely lose both. And when we saw her this August she explained that "we wanted some changes, you know. But we also wanted to keep so many of our own traditions, our own socialism."

Die Wende is the way the East Germans refer to November '89: "the turning." It's already part of the language, and already becoming encrusted with the mythology. Some will tell you that it was a vicious, suicidal last gesture by Honecker – or Egon Krenze – to destroy a failed socialism by flooding the land with *Deutschmarks,* all very Wagnerian. Some will tell you that in those last months concentration camps were being planned for the liberals in case the GDR survived. Some – and this is the really ugly part, and I'll get to it in a minute – will tell you it was the Jews. What all the *Wende* myths have in common is their sense of personal helplessness: *somebody* did *something,* and *we* have to pay.

I used to quarrel with Horst about this. The difference between Marx and Jesus, I'd insist, was that Marx was much the more trusting, innocent man. He *really believed* that if you set up the kinder, gentler society – and just enforced it for a while – people would just naturally get kind and gentle. It's Montessori metaphysics, and it's sweet. And it can kill you.

It can kill you because it tells you, at some deep level, that people never screw up. But they do. (The currently unfashionable name for this is "Original Sin," and that's all it means, really.) *We* do. When Celeste suggested to A. that, if she got sacked, *she* could find work as a teacher of English, A.'s response, no kidding was: "Well, maybe. But we're not used to making such plans for ourselves, you know." Well, yeah.

But there are always people who *will* make plans once the monitor has left the playground; people who are not kind or gentle at all.

A small illustration. One afternoon my stepson, Eric, and I were walking from our flat to the neighborhood grocery to get ol' stepdad some beer. And as we went through the pedestrian underpass we read the graffiti: swastikas, *Auslander Scheisse,* and of course the ever-popular *Juden Raus!* One graffito broke me up: a big spray-painted swastika with slogan, *Sieg Heiel!* "Dumb bastard can't even spell his own language," I laughed. "We don't have to worry about *him.*" And, "I think maybe we do," said Eric – as gravely as Horst himself could have done it. A wise kid, is my stepson.

This is not -- I repeat -- not one of those "German reunification means the fascist beast will rise from the ashes" pieces. For one thing, the fascist beast is everywhere. America certainly has enough lunatic Aryan-supremacy headbangers to get up a scratch basketball game (skinheads vs. brownshirts?) with the new Germany.

But in the GDR, until *die Wende,* that poison in the soul was denied, repressed by a system that, though partly corrupt and hopelessly artificial, nevertheless *thought* it could enforce a society where horror was no longer possible. That horror, the horror implicit in all moral choice (you *can* fall) was, besides VCR's and Marlboros, what the Wall kept out. Until very recently, all of Freud's work was forbidden in the GDR, which is both tragic and appropriate, since no one understood better than he the urge to deny the shadow in the self, and the terrible price of that denial.

One wanted to shout, sometimes, "But don't you *see*?" One didn't. Perhaps one should have. Auden's phrase keeps coming back to me: "Children afraid of the dark / Who have never been happy or good." So in the GDR the sons and daughters of the revolution – one of mankind's dreams -- have been granted their wish for escape, but with the condition that, the wish once granted, they can never have it back like it was.

The last day in Berlin, Celeste, Eric and I went to the Wall, at the Brandenburg Gate – once the center of this most melancholy of cities. The noble horses at the top of the Gate were gone. Some of the drunken celebrators of *die Wende*, it seems, had decided it would be a really keen idea to smash them. In what used to be no man's land were stalls selling sausage, beer – all West German -- and discarded Party pins, army decorations, and other GDR memorabilia. The garbage cans were overflowing and the flies were having the time of their lives, and there were even carriage rides available, at DM 5, around the old border. The Wall was still there but it had been chipped away for souvenirs and was about as noticeable as an umpire at a ballgame. There, Celeste, Eric, and I met A., Heike Schneider, a GDR journalist, Epi, her adopted black African son, and Gerlinde.

Gerlinde is forty-five, a devoted socialist, with the soul of a lotus blossom and the mind of a steel trap, and one of the very few people I have met to whom the word "lovely," properly applies. Celeste and A. and Heike all lined up in front of the Wall – on the Western side, of course – and I, Pentax at the ready, told Gerlinde to join them for a group photo.

And, "No," she said, looking at the remaining shards of the Wall. "It's just too – terrible."

And then I got it. It was about cigarettes. In '88, when I'd first crossed over to the West after two months in the *Hauptstadt*, I'd been shocked to see cigarettes thrown away only half smoked. We just didn't do that in the East: not because there was a shortage, and not because we couldn't afford more, but because, weirdly enough, the silly system we lived in under taught us not to *waste*. And on the Kurfursteindam they were buying cigarettes and smoking them halfway and didn't *know* what that *meant* to the people who were, for the sake of revolution, dragging it all the way down to the filter.

So Gerlinde said, "No- it's just too terrible," and I looked at the pavement and I saw hundreds of Marlboros and Kents and Dunhills half-smoked and tossed away. And I took a last drag on my Players, and I tossed that, too.

And that's how thick the Wall was.

IMAGES

1. MARZAHN

2. ADELHEID AND FRANK

3. Adelheid, George, Frank, Celeste and Eric

4. Epi, George and Eric

5. ERIC AND DEZSO

6. BRANDENBURG GATE FROM THE EAST

7. Brandenburg Gate from the West

8. Fulbrighters off the Wall

9. CHECKPOINT CHARLIE

10. THE WALL NEAR CHECKPOINT CHARLIE

11. No Man's Land

12. East Berlin from the Fernsehturm

13. STASI

14. MAY DAY PARADE

15. RUSSIAN EMBASSY

16. GERMAN TOILET

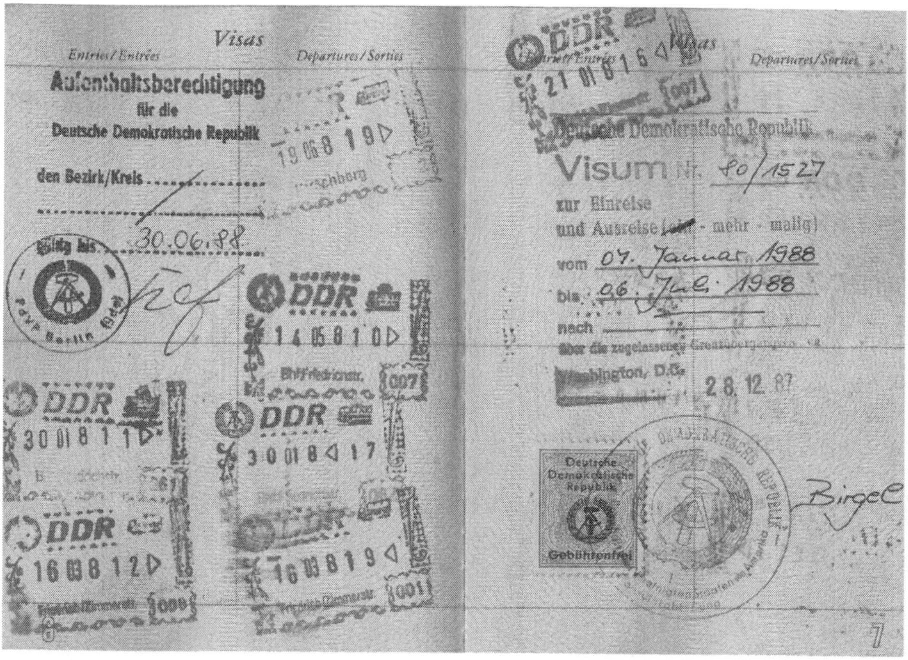

17. Passport Stamps

ABOUT THE AUTHORS

Celeste McConnell Barber teaches in the English Department at Santa Barbara City College and is the coordinator for the Great Books Curriculum on campus. She met her present husband, Ken Barber, in the Santa Barbara Cemetery while tending to Frank's grave, as Ken to his late wife's. She continues to travel, now captain to students, into the worlds of storytellers.

Eric Friedman received a B.A. in History from the University of Notre Dame and works in public policy for the County of Santa Barbara. Eric and his wife Julie have two sons, Henry and Charlie, and live in Santa Barbara, less than a mile from the home he left in 1988 on his way to Berlin.

16682663R00102

Made in the USA
San Bernardino, CA
14 November 2014